To C

INTERNATIONAL

"The Book That Lies Flat"
— *User Friendly Binding* —

This title has been bound using state-of-the-art **OtaBind®** technology.

- The spine is 3-5 times stronger than conventional perfect binding
- The book lies open flat, regardless of the page being read
- The spine floats freely and remains crease-free even with repeated use

We are pleased to be able to bring this new technology to our customers.

Health
Communications, Inc.

3201 S.W. 15th Street
Deerfield Beach, FL 33442-8190
(305) 360-0909

OTABIND®

INTERNATIONAL
The Netherlands

Other Books By Tian Dayton

Drama Games
Techniques For Self-Development

Moving On
Affirmations For Forgiveness
And Letting Go

AFFIRMATIONS
FOR PARENTS

How To Nurture Your Children
And Renew Yourself
During The Ups And Downs
Of Parenthood

Tian Dayton, M.A., A.M.S.

Health Communications, Inc.
Deerfield Beach, Florida

Tian Dayton, M.A., A.M.S.
Innerlook, Inc.
262 Central Park West
New York, New York 10024

©1992 Tian Dayton
ISBN 1-55874-151-8

Publisher: Health Communications, Inc.
          3201 S.W. 15th Street
          Deerfield Beach, FL 33442-8190

Cover design by Christine Clough

INTRODUCTION

Parents are a particularly wonderful breed of humans. We are the women sitting patiently in the corner of a baseball card store actually smiling while our son studies like a young Isaac Newton each player, each year, each hat. Or the father walking down 5th Avenue in a business suit unabashedly singing *Yankee Doodle Went To Town* because it is the only song his four-year-old daughter wants to hear. We are the men and women who cannot sleep at night when we are worried about our children — if something for them is not right. We are the mothers who go through the greatest pain of our lives and immediately afterward feel nothing but pure joy and gratitude for what that pain has brought. We are the people who would give up everything we have in exchange for our child, who strain and pray to learn to let go because letting go is so contrary to what our insides dictate, who feel more love looking into those beautiful little faces than we have ever felt, who like a mother partridge would court danger intentionally, rather than allow it to threaten our young, who know that there is really no such thing as quality time — it is all quality time. It is for these wonderful people that this book is written.

It all began a year ago triggered by a *Disco* party at our son's school. The parents were having dinner in one room and the kids were dancing in the other. My son was very excited and not particularly anxious; I, on the other hand, seemed completely unable to stop peeking in the door, asking him if he was having fun and talking to other parents about whether or not they thought the children were having fun. I was not just curious but momentarily obsessed with his experience and out of touch with my own. I had already gone through this period with my older daughter. If I could have shrunk myself to eraser size and gone to school with her in her pencil case, I would have. My urge to follow and control my children in sometimes unhealthy ways inspired me to sit down the morning after the dance and write out my feelings to gain some perspective. I began with the first of the 12 Steps, admitting that I was powerless over the

strength of my feelings for my children —
and the rest just came.

Nature has built into us tremendous feelings of protectiveness and nurturance so that we will tend and love these precious little lives that have magically come through us. If we did not have these feelings, perhaps we wouldn't be as completely attentive, but having them as we do, how do we separate what is functional and healthy dependence from what is dysfunctional and unhealthy co-dependence? Under the best of circumstances this is easy, but when we have had problems with co-dependent and enmeshed relationships in our own pasts, it becomes a particularly difficult task to separate the two. This book takes it a day at a time. In it I share my own experience, strength and hope, and perhaps some of it will fit for you.

Please take what you like and leave the rest.

God bless all our children!

SUGGESTED USES FOR THIS BOOK

1. *Parents in Recovery* — A daily guide and support for those who have grown up in dysfunctional homes, for changing behavior patterns in their own homes.
2. *Parent Support Groups* — A daily affirmation book for participants in parent support groups.
3. *Stimulation for Discussion* — In parenting groups an affirmation can be read and discussed by the group . . . or feelings that are brought up can be shared using the 12-Step model.
4. *As an easy reading book on parenting* — This can be a book simply to collect different ideas about parenting, to pick up and turn to any page for a quick and easy source of support.

For further workshop information in your area, contact: Tian Dayton, Innerlook Inc., 262 Central Park West, #4A, New York, N.Y. 10024 (212) 787-7914.

DEDICATION

To
Marina and Alex
with all my love

ACKNOWLEDGMENTS

I want to tell my parents that I love them unconditionally.

To my husband, Brandt: without you there would be no book. Thank you for our precious children — our love for one another — our family.

I wish to give my deep appreciation to Marie Stilkind and G.L. Mohan for their invaluable support and editorial work. They have made this book a joy to write.

EPIGRAPH

Children have never been very good at listening to their elders, but they have never failed to imitate them.

James Baldwin
"Fifth Avenue Uptown"
Nobody Knows My Name

*T*oday I understand that though I care for my children in a thousand different ways and have more impact on their lives than anyone, I remain essentially powerless. Who they are will ultimately be up to them. I can guide them, influence them and give them acceptance and love. I understand that my children were, are and always will be in God's hands. One of my important jobs as parent is to help them get in touch with their own internal healer, strength and Higher Power so that if they fall when I am not there to pick them up, they will be able to do that for themselves.

I accept my powerlessness
over my children.

Your children are not your children.
They are the sons and daughters of life's longing
  for itself.
They come through you but not from you.
And though they are with you, yet they belong
  not to you.

                                        Kahlil Gibran

Today I hold your hand and together we leap into life. Like children jumping into the deep end of a swimming pool and trusting the water to hold us up, I will trust life not to drop us. I believe that life means to be kind to us. I will do my part and have faith. I will not add on to the downside of my scorecard or use my list as a reason to hold back and cheat on life. I will live full out — I will give life the benefit of the doubt over and over and over again. I will recognize that all people have problems and we are no exception. I accept them as part of living. Just as I love my family with all their faults, I embrace life with all its trials.

Today I live full out.

He who would learn must suffer . . . against our will, comes wisdom to us by the awful Grace of God.

Aeschylus

I will look for humor in my day. I will cock my head to the side and gain a different perspective. If something is amusing, I will be tickled; if something is funny, I will laugh. Humor is a serious business, and those who really understand how to see and feel it have a kind of strength and energy to take to life that draws me to them. There is a quiet wisdom in humor, an acceptance of life and an ability to release us from the grip of a potential snare. I do not use humor inappropriately to mask feelings of hostility and to send double messages that I am not willing to take responsibility for. I see humor, appreciate it and share it at no one's expense.

I see humor in my day.

The love of truth lies at the root of much humor.

Robertson Davies

*T*oday I will let myself feel what *I* am feeling and let my children feel what *they* are feeling. So often I edit my feelings — some I decide are not good, some I would like not to be there at all. Some I am just tired of, so I try to cut and trim them according to what my mind tells me it would like to feel that day. Having done that, I set about to do the same with my children. Today I'll try something new. I'll pay attention to what each of us is feeling and give those feelings some respect and space. There's nothing so bad about them; they are only feelings and need not threaten me. I will pay attention to what I am feeling and what my children are feeling.

I respect my feelings.

Experience enables you to recognize a mistake when you make it again.

Franklin P. Jones

*T*oday I examine my need for drama in my life. I look at where I get hooked with my past and how that plays out in my present with my family today. Do I create more intensity than is necessary with my children? When they are upset by the normal frustration of growing up, am I able to see it for what it is, give it some space and move on, or do I read all kinds of deeper motives and agendas into their actions? If I do, I am probably bringing my past into my present and looking for drama to help me release the unresolved feelings I carry. Today I look into my need for drama in my life.

**I am willing to let go of
my need for drama.**

My argument is that War makes rattling good history; but Peace is poor reading.

Thomas Hardy

Today I will let my child separate from me knowing that without separation there can be no rapprochement. If I do not allow my child to leave, he cannot individuate and return to me for a new relationship in which we are no longer extensions of each other but individuals in our own right, reuniting in friendship and mutual respect. Separation does not happen all at once. It is a process of successfully leaving and returning that begins in early childhood. Over the years the child becomes able to take in a part of the parent within him and, in a sense, to parent himself. I will remain stable and easy to locate so that my child will be able to find me again. Gradually he will feel that same way about himself — that if he gets lost, he can always find himself again.

I honor my child's drive toward separation.

You may house their bodies but not their souls,
For their souls dwell in the house of tomorrow,
Which you cannot visit, not even in your dreams.

Kahlil Gibran

Today is my starting line. I had mistakenly perceived it as a finish line; I had to finish before I could begin. I had to have an emotional death before I could have an emotional life; a part of me had to end before I could begin again. I did not know that I was dragging death around within me nor that I had a right to leave it behind. I thought that to have a full life was asking too much — that to live free of abuse was unrealistically demanding, that to expect love was grandiose. Today I am graced with sanity and the understanding that life is to be loved and that love is to be embraced and felt.

Today is my starting line.

. . . In my end is my beginning . . .

T.S. Eliot

*T*oday I will resolve to clean house every day. Just as it is difficult to find what I need in a messy house, it is equally hard to find what I am looking for in a messy mind. Through quiet and meditation I need to deliver myself from all that pulls me down, keeps me preoccupied and, as a result, compulsive. This is a daily task and it is mine to find what works for me. Then and only then am I able to truly greet my child in the now. Whether it be through walking in nature, prayer, meditation or quiet relaxation, I will take the responsibility for cleaning out my own mind. The mind is a beautiful self-renewing entity always waiting patiently for light to be restored. Children go through this cleansing process naturally, so when I keep myself clear, I will be more naturally attuned with my child.

I cleanse my own mind.

Only our concept of time makes it possible for us to speak of the day of judgment by that name; in reality it is a summary court in perpetual session.

                                                    Franz Kafka

Today I stand up straight with my child. We are no better nor worse than anyone else. I align my energies not with the past or thoughts about myself that are painful and limiting, but with a loving universe. There are a thousand invisible hands waiting to lift my child and me up if I ask. For every one step I take toward God, God will take four toward me, they say. Today I believe that as hard as I have worked in my recovery, Grace has been an even more powerful force in my life. How my life has changed by surrendering and reaching upward! No one can keep me anywhere that I do not participate in being. I am no longer a victim of my childhood, and if I truly let my past go, then my child will have a better chance of being free.

We are children of a loving Universe.

No one can make you feel inferior without your consent.

Eleanor Roosevelt

I make peace with the past today. What I have not come to terms with in the form of unfinished anger, pain and resentment, I will pass on to my children and some day they will have to resolve it. I cannot change the past. Nothing I can do can alter anything that has already happened. I can, however, resolve not to make my present and future hostage to my past. Yesterday may be a die that is cast but today is a clean canvas. I can be as creative as my imagination and situation will allow. I can enjoy the feeling of creation that shines through me when I let it.

I am at peace with my past.

He had come to that time in his life (it varies for every man) when a human being gives himself over to his demon or to his genius, according to a mysterious law which orders him either to destroy or to surpass himself.

Marguerite Yourcenar

My children feel vulnerable. They are constantly being told what to do by adults. Sometimes the adults have their best interests in mind and sometimes they are just maintaining the status quo. I will keep all of this in mind when I talk to my children today. I won't just tell them what to do but I will talk over with them the reasons that I say what I do, along with sharing my own experience and understanding with them. I will not only teach them how to be but how to think and how to look at situations in a variety of ways. Children feel respected when they are talked to equally by adults and they learn to respect themselves.

**I will share my full thoughts
and listen to those of my children.**

Do not reason coldly with youth. Clothe your reason with a body if you would make it felt. Let the mind speak the language of the heart, that it may be understood.

Jean-Jacques Rousseau

Today I recognize that when I rush in to fix my child's problem too quickly, I keep him from feeling his own feelings. Whatever is going on with him, he needs to feel the feelings surrounding it in order to come to his own understanding and experience his own catharsis. He deserves his dignity. The anxiety that grips me when he is upset is *mine*. Removing *his* pain in an attempt to assuage my own is not fair, and it does not necessarily solve anything for him in the long run. If he is going to live successfully in the world, he will need to learn to deal with it realistically. I am there to protect and nurture him but not to live for him.

Today I fix myself before I fix my child.

He knows all about art but he doesn't know what he likes.

James Thurber

Today I recognize life for the constantly changing kaleidoscope of experience that it is. All is always in motion. All is energy in various forms. All is flux and movement and flow. To the extent that I can tune in with this reality, I feel a sense of peace. There is a stability in creating a raft for floating on the waters of change. I need not tire myself swimming against the current; I can let it work for me and my child, finding direction in existing direction and stability in what is already established. In my past, change became a threatening thing and I grew afraid of it. I can recognize this in myself and move on. I can learn to live with and even welcome life's changes.

I accommodate natural flux.

You could not step twice into the same river; for other waters are ever flowing on to you.

Heraclitus

Today I understand that I need to re-parent myself in order to be a good parent to my child. There are areas in which the parenting I got was not healthy for me. I need to go back to my own inner child and explore my feelings and fears to heal the wounds of my own childhood. I do not wish to pass these on to my children either in the form in which they were dealt to me, or as an overreaction, the opposite of what I got. Perhaps my parents were too lax with me and I felt abandoned. I may be too smothering with my children in an attempt to soothe my own inner child who still feels abandoned. I need to go back to the child within me and heal those wounds before I will be free to parent my child without an overhang from my own past.

**I will re-parent myself in
the light of today.**

*Life can only be understood backwards, but it must
be lived forwards.*

Albert Camus

Today I will not ask my children to be adults too soon. As I look back on my childhood I remember how overly responsible and serious I felt. I don't recall being carefree. Rather than wondering what game to play next, I worried about what was going on in my house when I wasn't there. I did not feel free to lose myself in the preoccupations of youth. Today I will honor my child's dreams. It is okay that she wonders what she wants to be and has lots of time to think about clothes and friends and the stuff of which childhood is made. There is nothing wrong with being young. Even if I was not always able to be a child myself, I am deeply grateful if I can give that to my child. It is healing for me to give to my child some of what I wish I had had because in giving it to her, I give it to myself as well.

I allow my child the preoccupations of childhood.

So do not ask for whom the bell tolls, it tolls for thee.

Ernest Hemingway

Today I will suspend judgment. I am always forcing myself to be strong and it is difficult for me to tolerate what I perceive as weakness in others. But isn't this in itself a weakness? Perhaps my strength would be more true if it were less brittle and more inclusive of the whole human condition. Maybe it isn't strength at all but fear of identifying with failure. Why am I so tough on myself and others? My children must feel it too. I wonder if they feel that they must always be brave and strong as I did. I wish that I could have crawled up on my parents' laps and been held for as long as it took to feel good again. I wish the vulnerability had not been shut down for fear of its taking over. Today I pray for real strength and tolerance within it.

**Today it is all right
to be afraid and feel weak.**

He jests at scars that never felt a wound . . .

William Shakespeare

Today I give up the need for intensity that is ultimately so draining. Growing up in a home where we needed intensity to feel alive and connected, I developed the habit of seeking it out and creating it in my home and in my relationships in the present. Today I trust that there are other ways that I can connect that are satisfying and fulfilling. My first connection needs to be between myself and my Higher Power. If I feel alive inside, I will not need to prove it to myself. This is a habit from my past that came out of my sense of isolation. Today I know how to be with myself and others without being drained; by accepting who I am and where I come from and by letting go of the kind of self-blame and hatred that keeps me antagonistic toward myself and others.

**I am alive and held
by life and my Higher Power.**

Consider the lilies of the field, how they grow; they do not toil, neither do they spin. And yet I say unto you, that even Solomon in all his glory was not arrayed like one of these.

The Bible

Today I recognize that children have a way of working things out that can be better than my way. They have a natural sense of how to restore balance and peace in their relationships that is appropriate for them. Sometimes a caring adult is needed to lend a hand but less often than I thought. My adult emotions can be inordinately heavy and complicated when I try to fit them into childhood interactions. Children do not perceive, process or think the way adults do. It doesn't work to force them to sound good and feel bad because they learn to say what they know I want to hear, but don't know why they are saying it. Then their inner reality is out of sync with the way they present themselves. Today I will spend more time observing and less time interfering.

**I respect my child's ability
to work things out.**

*I was born to know you. To give you your name
freedom.*

Paul Eluard

I will not force myself on my child today. I will understand that he has his own mind and will and that it is my job as his parent to help him recognize that within himself. He is capable of searching out and knowing his own truth if I let him. My position is not to stand in front of him and drag him through the life I have envisioned for him but to be a wind at his back and a friend to his heart. If I force my will on top of my child's, I may well get something that looks good at the moment but children aren't meant to look good; they are meant to grow. I want to help my child learn to know himself, to accept himself as he is, to build on and operate from his strengths and to understand his weaknesses.

**I allow my child to experience
his own life.**

The man who speaks the truth is always at ease.

Persian Proverb

*T*oday I see you as sent from God; sent as a reminder that at the very center of life is love and wonder and delight. When you laugh, I see rainbows and hear bells peal through the air. When you smile, the world feels happy. You teach me how to enjoy life through my love for you. I feel my soul is renewed. You make spirituality seem an everyday affair because my feelings for you bring me to another level of awareness of life. When I lay eyes on you, something deep within me says yes.

**You are precious beyond all words
and I see God in you.**

A woman without a child may have a house that shines but a woman with a child has a face that shines.

Indian Proverb

*T*oday I will not attempt to act as your inner voice. I will not answer questions for you, speak for you or tell you what you feel and think. My voice is so much louder and more practiced than yours and if I speak up quickly in your place, I will drown out the voice that is rising up within you. If I answer questions on your behalf, I will encourage you to be passive and I will be in little ways making you an extension of myself. I will listen today to what it is that you are trying to say and I will try to help you to find your own words. Then, when you have said it, I will congratulate you on a job well done!

**I really want to hear what
you have to say today.**

The truth is found when men are free to pursue it.

Franklin D. Roosevelt

Today I recognize that we are a part of one another. I accept it and I celebrate it. I feel deeply connected to you at some unquestioned assumed level. We were meant to know one another — it is as if we always did. When were you not a part of my life and heart? I will accept our presence in one another's life as meant to be. Together we have a chance to learn how to have relationships, to be fuller, happier, kinder people.

I am thine and thou art mine.

I am part of the sun as my life is part of me. That I am part of the earth my feet know perfectly, and my blood is part of the sea. My soul knows that I am part of the human race, my soul is an organic part of the great human race, as my spirit is part of my nation. In my own very self, I am part of my family.

D.H. Lawrence

Today I take pleasure in my life as it is. The greatest treasures in life lie in the stillness and awareness of the moment. Today I will not let the day just pass me by unnoticed. I will appreciate and enjoy what is in front of me and expand my consciousness into the now. My time with my child is limited and nothing I can do will ever bring these days back again. The days that I don't live today will not return. It takes spiritual strength to live with the knowledge that this is all there is for sure. The world need not disappoint me if I do not ask it to be what it cannot be or give me what it cannot give. It is I who assign meaning to my life and not the reverse.

I embrace your presence in my life today.

Blessed be childhood, which brings down something of heaven into the midst of our rough earthliness.

Henri Frederic Amiel

INTERNAL HEALER

January 24

*T*oday I will help you to access your own
internal healer. When you get a scratch,
I clean it and then I depend upon your body
to take over and heal itself. Isn't it the same
with your mind and heart? I can help you to
clean your wound by fully allowing you to
express your hurt, anger, frustration and
tears. Then, once your wound is clean, I will
trust the natural healing built into you to
take over and return you to a state of balance and health. I will work together with
the forces already present within you. I cannot do the whole job myself but if I do my
part well, giving you my full attention and
acceptance, the rest will take care of itself.

I trust your own internal healer.

*People's own wisdom will heal them; people's own
innate knowledge will bring them into balance.*

Chris Griscom

24

Today I will own my own shame and not pass it on to my children in the form of inhuman expectations. It is not the job of my children not to do what I did and my family did. They cannot make anything right for me; I have to make it right for myself. There are things from my past that I feel shame about. There were aspects of my family that I felt shame about. I will have the courage to change the things I can. I can face my own shame and share it with others and in this way begin to let it go. Maybe I couldn't get things to work within my family of origin; things working was an illusion that took all of our energy to maintain. I am not all-powerful. I can, however, face the past and let it go, giving my present the chance it deserves.

I feel and share my shameful feelings.

Blessed are they who heal us of self-despising.
Of all services which can be done to man,
I know of no more precious.

William Hale White

Today I want what I have. My life is already so full that if I could use and enjoy what is already mine, perhaps I would not feel such a need for more. The same goes with my children. Today I want and love what they already are. I am not engaged in a relationship with their potential but in a relationship with *them*. I can have dreams for them, but if I allow those dreams to superimpose themselves on what we have together today and create frustration within the relationship because we are not reaching them, I am selling the soul of our togetherness for a song. I will end up with neither the dream nor what we have now. People are not static packages; we are fluid expressions of life.

Today who you are is more than okay.

I do not read advertisements — I would spend all my time wanting things.

Robert Runcie

$\mathcal{T}$oday I value and understand the spiritual strength there is in solitude and I create it in my life. If I am mildly frantic or just slightly off center, I will try to find some quiet in my day to be alone, go deeply into myself and get in touch with my serenity. I will get less done on the outside and more done on the inside. Today I notice my child's need for solitude. When he is quiet and concentrating, I will not interrupt his silence. I recognize that he is moving toward a source within him, entering spontaneous meditation. I trust that if I let this happen over and over again without interfering, his tranquility will deepen and he will come to know his source of spirituality.

I allow my child to spend time in that deep and wordless place within him.

That inward eye which is the bliss of solitude.

William Wordsworth

Today I know that, much as I want to, I cannot control my children. I can only control myself and I know how difficult just doing that can be. I know that my children need my strength and guidance but my control is a very different thing. Today I will not make them the issue but will examine my own need to tell them who they are and what they should be. I will move one step closer toward giving my children their freedom by allowing them some space to discover themselves and what they like. I will deal with the anxiety that I carry with me from an unpredictable and often scary past on my own time so that I do not control the lives of my children to assuage my own discomfort at not knowing the outcome of a situation.

I recognize my need to control my children.

If there is a sin against life, it consists perhaps not as much in despairing of life as in hoping for another, and in eluding the implacable grandeur of this life.

Albert Camus

Today I will correct in myself what bothers me about my child. I will give my child a day off. What I see around me and in my interaction with those close to me is so often just a mirror reflection of my own state of mind and ability to relate. To always be blaming difficult interactions on my children is to miss the point. If I thoroughly examine my own side and alter my own behavior, the interaction will change. What am I seeing in my child may look only too familiar. Some difficult behavior is simply typical of childhood and adolescence and needs only to be recognized and understood. Other difficulties are connected to issues within me that get activated by my children but need to be understood in light of my own past experiences and their impact on me today.

Today I will look first at myself.

Take the log out of your own eye before you seek to remove the cinder from the eye of another.

The Bible

Today I recognize the importance of not interfering with my child's life until I have reflected on my own reaction to a given situation. Often when I have an unusually strong reponse to something that happened with my child, part of me wonders where it comes from. It is always difficult not to pass on the pain I grew up with. The unfinished business from my past makes my ability to tolerate what is happening with my child so low. Some of this is natural parental protectiveness and concern. Some of it is my own unresolved pain finding a place to roost. Somehow it seems more noble to suffer on behalf of my children than on my own behalf. But I do my children no favors by mixing my issues with theirs; it can only serve to train them in how to be co-dependent. Today I consider the situation first before I react.

I allow my child to find his own solution.

It is better to know some of the questions than all of the answers.

James Thurber

Today I am not afraid to try and fail. Failure is an illusion and a label that I no longer put my faith in. I see wisdom instead in the process of experimentation, understanding and clarification. If I do not move forward because of the fear of being proved wrong, I am missing the point. There are a thousand wrongs for every right by that philosophy, so what's the harm in just getting out there and trying? This is what I want for my children — for them just to stay engaged in the process. When I observe them playing, I understand that this is what children do naturally. I don't know when the concept of right and wrong will paralyze me or them, but today I do my best to affirm the process rather than the product.

I live in the experience of life, not the outcome.

No amount of experimentation can ever prove me right; a single experiment can prove me wrong.

Albert Einstein

Today I will not sell my life for a story of life. I will not have a love affair with who I could be, but who I am. Health sounds so easy and desirable in books and magazines. Recovery seems like the ultimate good mother that can solve all my problems in minutes and make me feel all better. If, however, I become infatuated with the idea of recovery at the expense of everyday common sense and honesty, I have won the battle and lost the war. This is a state disassociated from my real feelings, and my real feelings will surface sooner or later. They will come in disguised forms wearing masks or those things that I refuse to see in myself could be picked up and manifested in my children or in situations on which I project them.

**Today I manifest genuine health,
not phony recovery.**

That peculiar disease of intellectuals, that infatuation with ideas at the expense of experience that compels experience to conform to bookish preconceptions . . .

Archibald MacLeish

Today I return to a sense of innocence. The vulnerability we talk about in recovery — the willingness to feel our feelings as they are, rather than as we wish they were, to understand ourselves from within rather than from without — are all a part of innocence. Disease and compulsive desire seem to be connected to a loss of innocence and self. I often wonder how my children can find so much within the day to take joy in. Today I see that it is because they have so much within themselves. They feel that they are fascinating and beautiful. They are endlessly excited and amused with self-discovery. Today I understand that this is what spiritual recovery is all about. To keep alive to that current of life brings with it wisdom, guidance and innocence.

I tune in to another source.

And they were both naked, the man and his wife, and were not ashamed . . .

The Bible

Today I allow my imagination free flight and I observe your imagination as it moves from one thought to another. Why not entertain all sorts of possibilities? Life is full of small and big opportunities; sometimes just a little imagination is all it takes to make the difference between a dull and an interesting life. I can change my circumstances if I can imagine others. I can change my personality if I can imagine another way to be. Whatever feels stuck in me I can look at in my mind's eye and imagine alternatives. These are big challenges, but it is imagination that makes the little things in life richer — what to do with my day, how to dress, what to cook, what professional projects to explore. I will come to appreciate my own imagination and I will foster this in my child as well.

Inside my mind are endless possibilities.

Sometimes I've believed as many as six impossible things before breakfast.

Lewis Carroll

Today I will reverse roles with my child. I will attempt to see life from her perspective — through her eyes. I will do more than understand; I will actually change places with her in my mind, and through my imagination enter her experience of life. I cannot truly empathize with anyone unless I stand in their shoes. Today I will stand in my child's shoes. My ability to do this also reflects my willingness not to cling to my own position and to extend myself beyond my own limited view. If I can only know life from one perspective, my world will be narrow and my capacity to enjoy relationships will be lessened. Today I can and will do role reversals when I need to understand someone.

I can see things from another perspective.

I have found the best way to give advice to your children is to find out what they want and then advise them to do it.

Harry S Truman

Today I move myself out of your way. It is a great act of love on my part to let you work out the problems in your own life. I trust that you have a sense of how things operate best for you, and I love and respect you enough to allow you to experiment with your own approach to life. I can give you guidelines and unconditional love. I can encourage you to have the confidence to live your own life, but I cannot live your life for you. Ultimately you will have to work things out for yourself, and the more practice you get at that while you are young, the better you will be able to face life on your own; each day, a little more.

I love you and I let you work things out on your own.

Whenever we are doing for the child what the child can easily do for himself, we are in the way of his development.

Maria Montessori

Today I respect myself for my perseverance. Slow and steady wins the race. As I mature I come to understand and appreciate the value in working at things steadily and sincerely. Everyday life has a gentle comforting rhythm that I appreciate. Daily tasks regularly performed with love have a beauty all their own. This is what I want my child to see and to come to know — that there is a quiet strength and majesty in a simple life well lived. Much can be perceived when I take my time; there is so much to see if I really look. I value steadiness and a regular life. Little by little, one day at a time, I give this gift to my children.

I see beauty in small everyday acts.

A small daily task, if it be really daily, will beat the labors of a spasmodic Hercules.

Anthony Trollope

*T*oday I let go and allow God to do the work. I clear up in my own mind what I would like to see in my relationship with my child and I simply release that understanding with full faith that my sincere thoughts have a power of their own. If I am experiencing difficulty at this stage with my child, I will visualize the way I would like it to be and that is what I will see in the place of my negative thoughts. If I would like something for him, I will visualize that. I will substitute positive thoughts for any negative ones I hold about my child and unconsciously project onto him.

I acknowledge the power of my thoughts.

As water by cooling and condensation becomes ice, so thought by condensation assumes physical form.

Paramahansa Yogananda

Today I do not notice in my children what I should be noticing in myself. I will not ask them to correct in themselves what needs correcting in me. This is a subtle way of passing on the pain — to see all sorts of areas for improvement in them and to be constantly "working on them." Let me work on myself instead and observe how magically my worries for them clear up. Often my concerns for my children are a projection of my own unresolved issues that I refuse to see in myself. My drive for their success may reflect my own frustration at not having been more successful. My need to overparent them or parent them perfectly may speak to the inadequate parenting and sense of abandonment I experienced as a child.

**Today I look at myself first
and my child next.**

*Not in the shouts and plaudits of the throng,
But in ourselves are triumph and defeat.*

Henry Wadsworth Longfellow

*T*oday I find you amusing. In your efforts to learn about the world you do things that touch my funny bone. You have a sweet humor about you that charms me. You see humor in things that I miss. Today I will see what you see. I appreciate the lightness that you are capable of bringing into my life if I let you, and how you shift my perception from a hundred other places into the moment. Sometimes I dwell on my responsibilities and worries but today I will let you make me laugh and feel my spirit renewed by yours.

I let you bring lightness into my heart.

may my heart always be open to little birds
who are the secrets of living
whatever they sing is better than to know
and if men should not hear them, men are old

may my mind stroll about hungry and fearless and
thirsty and supple
and even if it's sunday may I be wrong
for whenever men are right they are not young

e e cummings

Today I will visualize in my mind's eye good things for myself and my children. I will actually imagine what I want in my life as being already here. I will participate in my inner dream as if it were reality. I will taste it, smell it, see it and believe it. Seeing is believing, and believing is seeing. There is more than enough room in life for all of us to have what we want. If good things happen for others, why not for me and my children? I will take a risk in my imagination today and envision what I would like to see in my child's life and in my life. I have nothing to lose by trying.

It's fun to visualize our good.

Beholding beauty with the eye of the mind, he will be enabled to bring forth, not images of beauty, but realities (for he has hold not of an image but of a reality).

Plato

*T*oday I recognize you as unique and one of a kind. Like anything in nature there are no two of you, just you — as you are, your own child. Everything you are or will become is filtered through a combination of characteristics and attitudes that are exclusively yours. You, therefore, will not do anything that is not an original reflection of yourself. Rather than wanting you to be like anyone else, I will love and appreciate you just as you are. You have your own gifts and it is my job to help you to recognize and build on these strengths. In this way you will come to appreciate yourself and what you have to give to the world.

**There is only one of you —
you are an original.**

Whatever you do, try to do it as nobody else has done it before.

Swami Sri Yukteswar

Today I look at you and I see the kind heart of a loving God. You came not just through my body but through my soul. You are evidence of the mystery of life, and for all our scientific accomplishments today, we know nothing of how we really come here. At best we can document but even there we fall short. There are those who say they don't believe in a Higher Power — they need proof — but aren't they themselves the proof they are seeking? Every leaf, every flower and tree, every human form — we can trace their biological origins but without the mystery of life and breath, they are only shells. Everywhere there is evidence of God and mystery in my life, and most mysterious of all is you.

I embrace mystery in my life.

Love, you are love, better far than any metaphor can ever ever be.
Love, you are love, my mystery — this mystery of love . . .

The Fantastiks

*T*oday I will be ordinary. I will be pleased by little things — my morning coffee, breakfast together, something amusing that you say. Today I will not pretend anything or wish for what I do not already possess. It is enough for me just to be here with you, for you to be here with me and to walk through my day with awareness and love. Everyday life is beautiful and somehow the older I get, the more it is simple pleasures that bring me real joy. I like to accomplish things in their own time without a lot of pressure so that I can enjoy the process. I feel less demanding of life and more able to *let* my child grow up, rather than *make* him grow up. The pressure I exert on his life gets neither of us anywhere; it is fear-based.

I let little things please me.

Who sees me in all
And sees all in me,
For him I am not lost,
And he is not lost for me.

Bhagavad Gita

Today I take strength and comfort from the order that exists. If nature attends to each and every detail of the universe with such evident care and precision, then why not me and my family? As random as life can seem, there is a rhythm and a plan. I welcome the recognition of powerlessness that is a part of living with nature. I cannot control nature, only accept it. When I go with the flow, there is something in the quality of my day that changes. When my mind is overly full, nothing good comes of it; it's just a sort of mental traffic jam. I will take my example from the order of nature.

**I trust that there is a pattern and
a truth behind what I see.**

*Nature is full of genius, full of divinity — so that
not one snowflake escapes its fashioning hand.*

Henry David Thoreau

*T*oday I realize that I draw negative people and situations into my life in order to heal my deep hidden fears in the present. I unconsciously recreate them. When people come to represent something or someone for me from my past and activate these feelings, it gives me a chance to make them conscious and deal with them. In a funny way I can be grateful for these life occurrences because any fear I face and heal releases more of my personal energy that I can then use in my life and my parenting. I have more to give my children when fear is not preoccupying me unconsciously. I am open to working out my fears the way life presents them.

I work out my deepest fears.

We two kept house,
The Past and I, The Past and I;
I tended while it hovered nigh,
Leaving me never alone.

Thomas Hardy

Today I will simplify my life. Whatever state it is in, I can simplify it more. One of the great lessons of spirituality is in simplicity — it is the gateway to a tranquil mind. I observe that when my own life is in order, the lives of my family seem less complicated too. Somehow the demands of family life fall into place more easily if I am not trying to do too much. My disease of co-dependency has told me that I don't have the right to say no; that I must do everything anyone expects of me. Today I know that *no is a complete sentence* and an absolutely necessary one if I am to take control of my own life. In fact it's a beautiful word. It gives me back to myself. Yesterday that would have been a frightening thought; today I can manage it.

Keep it simple.

I have come back to where I belong; not an enchanted place, but the walls are strong.

Dorothy H. Rath

I remember today that I really did not always get to be a child. When my children act like children, I don't always know what they're doing. I don't remember acting like that myself. I was much more concerned with my parents' feelings than my children seem with mine. Sometimes I resent their not wanting to take care of me. Now I wonder if I am on the right track in my thinking. Maybe part of my concern was a preoccupation with the moods of my parents because I was secretly afraid of them. It may be that my children feel more free to say what they feel because they are less afraid of me. Perhaps my children don't feel that they need to take care of me by denying their own truth. I remember how much I would have liked to speak my mind as a child and I am glad that my children are free to speak theirs.

I allow my children to speak their minds.

Waste not fresh tears over old griefs.

Euripides

Today I accept the shame I carry around with me from my childhood and I see how it affects my life. It is difficult for me to allow stability and happiness to be the norm in my life when I don't feel worthy of them. I felt that my family had shame-filled secrets and that if other people knew these, they wouldn't like us anymore. So I kept my silence and hid my shame where no one could see it, not even I. I felt isolated in my feelings of inadequacy because I feared that in showing them I might be rejected. I made myself appear strong as a defense against this inner doubt. Today I know that inner doubt is a part of the human condition. I am learning to experience my feelings of shame and acknowledge them so that my children may not pick up on them and internalize them as their own. I am able to share these feelings with others and make the connections I denied myself.

I experience my shame and allow it to lift.

Mankind must remember that peace is not God's gift to his creatures; peace is our gift to each other.

Elie Wiesel

I will allow sickness to leave my home. Co-dependency has a life of its own. It lives in and around human beings. It wants to have the last word, to dictate terms, to control. It wants to hold the emotional purse strings, to call the shots. I do not need to do that or live with that today. Yesterday I didn't know better but today I do. I am learning about a new way of living where everyone wins. I used to think there had to be a winner and a loser. Today that seems silly. There is more than enough room for everyone to have their emotional space without trampling on each other. When this is not happening, I will step back and re-examine. We no longer have to live with sickness in our home.

**I let go of the hold disease
had on my life.**

*How dreadful knowledge of the truth can be when
there's no help in truth.*

Sophocles

Today I will ". . . Be still and know that I am God . . . ." I will join with the moment and await its lessons. I know when I am tense and cannot think clearly that I have to take myself home, quiet down and give myself all the hours I need until I relax. When I am tightly wound, my whole perception of the world is different. I react to things my child does in a way that I would never react if I were relaxed. What is the point of letting myself get tense? Who does it benefit? Not me and certainly not my child. I will take the time I need to feel quiet inside.

I give myself the gift of time.

You do not leave your room. Remain sitting at your table and listen. Do not even listen, simply wait. Do not even wait, be quite still and solitary. The world will freely offer itself to you to be unmasked, it has no choice, it will roll in ecstasy at your feet.

Franz Kafka

Today I will not push to have things my way. Pushing throws the tender eco-system of relationships out of balance. I cease to get an accurate picture of the subtle ins and outs of the family when I try to control activities and outcomes. Naturally, as parent I need to make plans and take charge but I don't have to take this role and run with it. Sometimes this extends into my writing an agenda or a script for others, feeling that they should follow it. Unfortunately, in the process of scripting everyone else's life, I forget to write one for my own. I am left with an empty and neglected feeling and I begin to resent my children. Today I will start to reverse this process and see how it feels.

I stop and step back before I push.

The balance of power.

Sir Robert Walpole

I know I cannot hold you forever. I have borrowed you from life for a few years to keep me company. This time spent with you is precious and I know that when you grow up, a part of me will miss these rich and beautiful moments we have together. But that is the way of life and I trust that when the day comes, we will both be ready for it. I hope you will consider me a close and deeply committed person in your life, that you will count me among your nearest and dearest friends. As for me I will ever carry you in my heart.

I cherish my time with you.

Like a kite
Cut from the string
Lightly the soul of my youth
Has taken flight.

Ishikawa Takuboku

Today I will observe the natural restlessness of my mind — how it desires to fly from thing to thing. I will see that my mind takes off easily but does not always know how to land. How can I hope for peace in my home and calm with my children when my own mind is flying all over the place? I'm not sure that this is due to living in modern society; I think it is just the nature of the mind. The more my mind flies all around, the less time it spends focused within. Its focus is on external objects; this is co-dependency — the flight from self. Today I will quietly bring my mental energy to where it belongs — back to me. Until I do this, I will not be in a position to really be with my children and they will feel it too. I need to first be with myself and then with my children.

I will gently call my mind back to me.

There are many truths of which the full meaning cannot be realized until personal experience has brought it home.

John Stuart Mill

Today I release my child from my expectations. He has a right to be who he is and not what I want him to be. I have so many ideas of what I want for my child, what I want him to do for a living, who I would like him to marry. There are also many things I want him to do now — play sports, have certain friends, get good grades. I sometimes put him on a track to where I want him to go. I am not sure today if he will be able to find himself buried underneath the pile of my plans for him. It occurs to me today that he may have some plans for himself. I will listen to what my child seems to like on his own.

**I lift some of my expectations
from my child.**

How many cares one loses when one decides not to be something but to be someone.

Coco Chanel

*T*oday I loosen my grip of power over you. I am so big compared to you that I forget you are like a human living among giants. Even the house must look huge. I remember how things seemed when I was small. When I go back and visit the places that were so grand to me in childhood, they look so different, as if they had shrunk both in stature and importance. I need to remember that my relationship to you gives me power that I do not necessarily feel that I have. I need to remember how big I feel to you and modify my actions accordingly.

I take responsibility for my power over you.

We thought because we had power, we had wisdom.

Stephen Vincent Benet

Today I listen to my own pain and my child's pain. Pain is diagnostic. If something hurts it means that there is an unseen wound or that I have exceeded my capacity and it's time to stop. I can increase my tolerance only by slow and gradual expansion, not by doing everything all at once. When my child seems to experience pain, I will stop pushing. There is really no rush. My child will need time to grow up. Pushing him through his developmental stages will only make more work for him later because he will have to find a way to fill in the missing pieces. We each have a right to the time that we need to grow.

I will listen to pain's message.

Education is the ability to listen to almost anything without losing your temper or your self-confidence.

Robert Frost

Today I acknowledge the power of my own past. I had parents and I am a parent. My greatest lessons in parenting are the ways in which I was parented. No matter how enlightened I am in terms of modern information, I am rendered powerless when feelings from my own past take over. I owe it to myself and my children to heal past wounds so that I do not pass on the pain. It is what I do, not what I say, that my children take in. They naturally look up to me and use me as their primary teacher in life. How do I feel about myself and what am I showing to my children. What am I teaching them about how to be? Am I willing to be honest with them about my shortcomings and am I showing them that I can look at myself, work on myself and make significant changes?

I can heal past wounds.

The gods visit the sins of the father upon the children.

Euripides

Today I remember ". . . Gather ye rose-buds while ye may . . ." It's a beautiful day, we are alive, we have each other and that is enough. We have every opportunity to make this day beautiful if we choose to. Why is this day any different from any other? I have enjoyed countless days and felt a beautiful spiritual energy present. Why is this day not the same? What if I give it a try? I will open myself to the beauty available today. Then when I feel it within me, I will share it with you. You are part of this day of possibilities, though oftentimes you seem much more aware of them than I am. You really do find life exciting, don't you?

I am here for life.

My advice to you is not to inquire why or whither, but just enjoy your ice cream while it's on your plate — that's my philosophy.

Thornton Wilder

I will let you get love, support and nurturing from outside. I know that the world has so much to give my children. I am not able to meet all of their needs nor should I be able to. That is what other people are in their lives for. I will do them a real favor if I allow them to bond and form meaningful relationships with others. I know that there is no need for me to feel threatened by this as if I will be supplanted in their hearts; I trust that my place is assured. I delight in seeing my children able to meet their needs from a variety of sources. In this way I am teaching them that it is safe and fulfilling to reach out.

**I let my children form
meaningful relationships outside myself.**

*Consider the little mouse, how sagacious an animal
it is which never entrusts its life to one hole only.*

Titus Plautus

Today I will let myself go with the flow. I will take the path of least resistance and see where it leads me. Today I don't feel the need to impose a thousand tiny adjustments on my day. I feel like avoiding obstacles, not creating them. Slowly, slowly wins the race. There is a lot to life that I miss when I get controlling; there is a lot of you I miss. I can't afford that waste of time and energy now. I need all of my resources present to enjoy the moment with you. There are many things in my life that I can do nothing about. Today I recognize that and I really let myself not strain to solve the unsolvable.

I am grateful to feel powerless.

The wind said
You know I'm
The result of
Forces beyond my control.

A.R. Ammons

Today I make peace within the vicissitudes of life. When I grew up, we all tried so hard to be perfect — to present the face of a completely successful family to the world. This is just not real. It's no wonder that I had a vague sense of something being off all the time. I am okay today with life being a constantly changing experience. I don't feel that driving need to fit it all into a big box with a ribbon and a smile on top. I appreciate it for all its beauty and I understand that if I cut myself off from sorrow, I cut myself off from joy as well. In my family today it is all right to feel. My children don't have to bear the burden of proving to me that I am a good parent by being perfect themselves. They can be who they are.

I allow myself and my children to be real.

I would that my life remain a tear and a smile.
A tear to unite me with those of a broken heart;
A smile to be a sign of joy in my existence.

                                        Kahlil Gibran

I take pride in my child today. I know that pride can get people into trouble — that hubris is to be sidestepped — but to tell the truth, when I look at my child, my heart bursts with parental pride. Not that I feel I have made this person or own her, but it is undeniable that she has come through me and she is flesh of my flesh. I adore her. She is evidence of the most creative moment of my life and each day with her is new creation, a new beginning. What an opportunity to throw myself into life fully, with your boundless energy and my accumulated wisdom and knowledge of the world. We make a great team you and I — we can really dance.

I take pride in this wondrous child.

The truly proud man is satisfied with his good opinion, and does not seek to make converts.

William Hazlitt

Today I live like a spiritual warrior in the presence of God. I do not underestimate my power to influence my life in a positive way. My thoughts themselves have power. My beliefs are doors that open up to experience. I choose to have positive beliefs in relationship to myself and my child. If I want something for my child, I will hold him in a positive light and believe fully that he is capable and confident. I imagine my child happy and well-adjusted. I hold my family in light and love and assume that good is in store for us. I take for granted that my family is normal and healthy and that we love and support one another.

I believe that life will be good to me and mine.

No one can harm you if you truly believe in God; when you believe in the negative thought that somebody is injuring you, you give them the power to do so.

Paramahansa Yogananda

*T*oday I will embrace change. I know that change is the only true constant of life and today I will not resist it. I will let change happen. If I cling to the past, I will distort my present and if I fight change in the now, I will postpone my future. Everything in nature changes — the seasons, the water levels, grass, leaves, wind, fruits and vegetables. Nature is in a constant state of flux and change and without this, there would be no growth. My child and I are a part of nature too. We do not need to force change; it happens by itself. Ours is to allow it and in this way we grow.

I allow change to happen.

All is flux, nothing stays still . . . Nothing endures but change.

Heraclitus

Today I will remember how important the environment I create for you is. I am in a position to have such a strong impact on your life. I am creating the home that you grow up in. I am your parent — a co-creator in the development of you. I provide your home, cook your food, designate your school, set rules and entertainment. I take you traveling, to friends' houses, to classes. I am such a powerful presence in your young life. I need to remember how formative my influence on you is. Today I will create a friendly comfortable supportive world for you to grow up in.

I am a very important person in your life.

There is no creature whose inward being is so strong that it is not greatly determined by what lies outside of it.

George Eliot

Today rather than tell you what is in my mind, I will wonder what is in yours. Instead of simply telling you what to do, I will attempt to get a sense from you of what you wish to do. I know that becoming familiar with your own personal preferences and being allowed to voice them helps you to get to know yourself and if I make room for you to do this, your self-concept and self-confidence will rise. I am not you and you are not me. I cannot assume that you will like everything I have in mind for you, nor that I will like all that you have in mind for yourself. We can work together, though, to find a common ground where we both feel comfortable.

I support you in learning about yourself.

And I perpetually await a rebirth of wonder.

Lawrence Ferlinghetti

*T*oday I expect the best for you. No more gloom and doom projections onto your life. If I begin to think negatively about your life, I will look into my own past and present attitudes about myself to understand why I need to think that way about you. You are not me and there is no need to assign my own insecurities and fears to you. I hold you in my mind's eye as a success. I envision good things coming your way. I feel that life wishes to treat you well. I assume that you will have what it takes to be happy and comfortable with yourself and others.

All is right in your world.

Could it be, yes it could, somethin's coming, somethin' good, if I can wait.

West Side Story

Today I will give my child something I did not get myself. It can be so painful for me to give what I myself did not receive. It feels easier to pass on what I got in a knee-jerk reaction, whether or not it helped me as a child. Today I will examine one of those reactions I pass on to my child that I would like to change. I will let my mind float to the past and come in touch with where it began and how it felt. I will feel all of those feelings and let them go. Now I will put something good in its place. I will imagine the way I would have liked it to be. I will see what I wish I had had at the time and that is what I will pass on to my child today.

I will stretch myself today.

You give little when you give of your possessions. It is when you give of yourself that you truly give.

Kahlil Gibran

I will set boundaries for you today. I will neither make them too rigid, making you feel like a caged animal, nor will I make them too lax and ill-defined, making you feel abandoned. I am willing to truly spend time examining your needs and my own, and I will set boundaries that are thoughtful and considerate. The boundaries I give you are meant to keep you safe, not to frustrate you or lord it over you. The boundaries I set for myself are a form of self-caring — they are what allow me to operate safely in the world while keeping myself intact. I will set boundaries for you and slowly help you to learn to create them for yourself.

I am willing to set appropriate boundaries.

License is freedom without destiny.

Fyodor Dostoevsky

Today I trust. I trust the moment, I trust the hour, I trust the day. I trust that life is inherently good and that the world means to do no harm to me or my child. I trust in my ability to be a parent and in my child's ability to be a person. I trust that if I let go, my world will not fall apart. I trust the sun to rise in the morning, set in the evening and the seasons to follow one another. I trust that I will have what it takes to get through and that if I release my child to his Higher Power, he will be held. I trust my feelings to be right for me and my child's to be right for him. I trust my child.

I am where I am meant to be.

As I watched the sea gulls I thought: That's the road to take; find the absolute rhythm and follow it with absolute trust.

Nikos Kazantzakis

Today I release your spirit. I know that I do not own you. I cannot keep you by holding on to you. People are not belongings and you are not my possession. Though I refer to you as mine, I know that I mean it only in a limited way. You are not mine and I am not yours — we belong to life and our own individualized paths. We are here to support and help each other, to learn from one another. It is no accident that we are together. I do not wish to be the final port in your journey but a harbor from which you are free to come and go.

You are a free spirit.

Into thy hands, Lord, I commend my spirit.

The Bible

I will tell my child I love him today. In fact I will send him affirming messages every chance I get. Each affirmation I give my child will travel to his unconscious mind and enter his storehouse of good feelings about himself. My child looks up to me and trusts me. When I tell him he is wonderful, he believes it. Life is long and the world can be difficult, so I will send my child into it armed with my good opinion. I know that every good thing I say to my child adds up inside of him and I will keep saying them every chance I get.

I affirm my child over and over.

*Love that is hoarded, moulds at last until we know
    one day . . .
The only thing we ever have is what we give
    away . . .*

Emily Dickinson

Today I will let you have your own truth
and I will have mine. Few things in life
are as important as knowing what your own
truth is. It is so easy with children to think
that our truth is or should be theirs; but
why should it be? They really are with us
such a short time, and if they have to live
the rest of their lives with our truth, something will never feel quite right to them —
like wearing a suit that doesn't quite fit. We
have good ideas for our children and plans
that will serve them well certainly, but as to
an intimate personal truth, wouldn't they be
better off in life with their own?

God Bless the Child that's got his own.
Billie Holiday

*This above all: to thine own self be true
And it must follow, as the night the day,
Thou canst not then be false to any man.*

William Shakespeare

You have your own blueprint for life inside of you. Like a flower that grows from a seed mysteriously into something with grace, color and beauty, you pass through your developmental stages as if you had read some book on how to look and behave. How does this happen? How do you know that you are supposed to be doing these things that you do? I marvel at you. Watching you grow up is like watching some wondrous garden bloom. You enter this dance of life with such natural enthusiasm as if you knew you belonged here. Today I will just stand back and observe you as I would observe a sunset or a group of trees in the wind. You are a thing of true beauty full of mystery and I love to watch you.

I marvel at the wonder that is you.

A thing of beauty is a joy forever:
Its loveliness increases;
It will never pass into nothingness.

John Keats

When I grew up, I learned not to rock the boat; asserting my own opinions and desires could get me in trouble. Sometimes I carry this over in my parenting; I don't take a stand or set limits. When my children push or threaten to get angry, the fear I felt as a child comes up and my reaction is to placate them and keep the peace. This is not healthy for my children because it trains them to push and throw tantrums to get what they want. I need to feel those fears I felt as a child along with the sense of helplessness that overwhelmed me. I need to separate myself as a child from myself as an adult. I also need to separate my inner child from the child I am raising.

I am able to separate past from present.

Loving a child doesn't mean giving in to all his whims; to love him is to bring out the best in him, to teach him to love what is difficult.

Nadia Boulanger

Today I am able to be responsible for my own actions. I do not need to make my children responsible for what I do. My children cannot make me do anything I do not let myself do. When I make them feel that they have that kind of control over me, I frighten them. It is scary for kids to feel that they are in control of their parents. They are at peace when their parents are in charge of themselves and the family. Children should always be consulted and listened to but the responsibility for their parents and family ought not to lie with them. Their job is to learn to be responsible for themselves. They can do that if we help them, give them a chance and set the example.

I am fully responsible for my actions.

I know of no more encouraging fact than the unquestionable ability of man to elevate his life by a conscious endeavor.

Henry David Thoreau

Today I will trust that things will turn out all right if I let them. Rejection and abandonment were very real for me when I was young. Whenever I feel those feelings today, or worse, I am afraid that my child is feeling them. I will take a moment to tune in and see what might be going on inside of me. I have a very hard time not walking around feeling a quiet fear and panic. Today I understand that things can work out — times have changed. My children are not me; they have grown up in a very different atmosphere from the one I grew up in. When I feel sorry for them, is it really their pain I am feeling or my own? I can let life work out.

I trust situations to work out.

To every season — turn, turn, — turn.
There is a reason — turn turn.

The Bible

I will "act as if" today. If I am not everything that I want you to have in a parent
today, I will dare to "act as if" I am. I have to
start somewhere and I want so much for
you to have a healthy confident parent.
Some situations scare me and make me insecure but I will handle them. I will not use
my insecurities as an excuse not to try.
Sometimes just moving from fear into action
is enough. When I move through my own
fear, I surprise myself. I am capable of more
than I previously thought I was. Today when
I feel that old inertia coming over me, I will
make a move in a positive direction.

I can do more than I think I can.

The only thing we have to fear is fear itself.

Franklin Delano Roosevelt

Just as I watch a summer wind rustle the leaves of the trees and appreciate its beauty, or sit on the bank of a river as it finds its way over and around rocks and branches, so I will watch you today with no more thought of controlling you than I would attempt to interfere with the wind and the water. You too are a part of nature and come with an inherent program for life. I do not teach you to breathe or make sound or move your body. I have to depend on what you bring with you inside for all of these things. You know when you are hungry — I do not — and you know when you are full. It is you who knows where and how much it hurts and what brings you joy. Today I will watch you unfold before me, knowing that you have a plan for life within you.

I will watch and look and listen in awe.

A child said "What is the grass?"
  fetching it to me with full hands;
How could I answer the child?
  I do not know what it is anymore than he.

Walt Whitman

Today I recall what it was like to feel loved and special as a small child. Because I lost this, it is almost too painful to remember, but recovery is about giving me back to myself and working through the pain so that I can once again feel the pleasure. The loss that I have felt, and on top of that the denial of that loss, has made me a complicated person emotionally. Today I am not afraid to remember the richness and beauty that I experienced with my parents. I remember how completely I loved and trusted them. How powerful and omnipotent they seemed to me! How safe I felt in their presence! It is true that I became disillusioned but I no longer need to let the sadness of that keep me from some of my fondest and most cherished memories. I recall with love and gratitude the beauty that was mine.

I treasure the joy.

God grant you one face there you loved when all was young.

Charles Kingsley

I will not jump ahead of you today. I will meet you where you are. Why rush? There is time enough to be a grown-up. Pushing and moving too quickly will not make you a better one. In fact being fully where you are today will allow the next stage to happen more easily. It is a beautiful thing to be young, to look forward each day to growing taller, learning new things, doing tasks that yesterday were impossible. Growing is so full of excitement and rushing it only denies the pleasure and the celebration that accompany inner and outer movement. Today I find that where you are in your journey is a good place to be.

I give you all the time you need to grow.

Events will take their course, it is no good our being angry at them; he is happiest who wisely turns them to the best account.

Euripides

Today I will understand that my version of quality time may not be yours. Your quality time may be five minutes of intense sharing after school, a walk to the park, a shared hot dog on the street, shopping together or baking cookies. I will not be led by trends but will trust my own instincts to know how to spend time with you. Isn't it also quality time when we are in separate rooms doing different things with the peaceful, secure feeling of having each other near at hand? Today I know that quality time is understood time — felt time when we somehow know that even though we aren't doing anything special, it feels special. Today I recognize time as it happens and the inherent quality within it.

**Time with you has a special
quality all its own.**

Time for a little something.

A.A. Milne

Today I will see you not as a youngster with actions motivated only by the moment, but as a child working hard to build yourself into the person you someday will be. You are the sum of all your parts and each part of you that you build well today will be your foundation as a person. Growing up is not full of moments lost. Whether we remember our young years or not, they are filled with learning and experiences that create us. A well-laid foundation provides a sound structure upon which to build. If the foundation is strong, the building will stand. If you get enough of what you need in your childhood, you will have what it takes to actually live your life.

**I see you as building
the person you are to become.**

Rat said, "You're a wonder! A real wonder, that's what you are. I see it all now! . . ."

Kenneth Grahame

I will finish my own business today. If I do not deal with my own problems and complexes, I will pass them on to you either by omission or commission. If I try to keep you safe from unresolved sides of myself, I will be holding important parts of me from you and you will wonder what I am hiding. If I release problems inappropriately, you will feel that you are the cause of them and because you will be unable to make things better, you will grow up with a quiet despair. The only way I can keep you free from my "stuff" is to free myself of it. That will take work on my part but it is the greatest gift that I can give you.

**Today I take care of business —
first things first.**

I read part of it all the way through.

Samuel Goldwyn

Today I will not judge you. Oftentimes I catch myself criticizing you in small ways, nitpicking and getting on your back for little things. If you acted toward me the way I do toward you, I would probably not like it. Today I will remember that who I am is the deepest message I send to you. If I want you to be a particular way, the method of teaching you that is to be it myself. If I want you to be kind, I need to treat you and others with kindness. If I want you to be even tempered, I have to show you what that means by my own behavior. Today I understand that "do as I say, not as I do . . ." doesn't work. Actions speak louder than words. Today I am willing to be the kind of person I tell you to be.

I will talk less and do more.

We have learned that we cannot live alone, at peace; that our well-being is dependent on the well-being of other nations.

Franklin D. Roosevelt

Today I will be genuine. When I talk to you, I will be real — I will let you know who I am inside. Often I hold back with you because I am more tied to the role of being a parent than being me; I become afraid that I will say too much or cross boundaries inappropriately. Today I am confident that I know enough about healthy parenting to be myself with you and still remain a proper parent. I do not need to go into details about myself that you aren't interested in, but I can still share my honest thoughts and feelings with you. I will not use you as my confidante nor will I estrange myself from you by keeping too much distance.

**I can be myself with you and
remain appropriate.**

*Not what we give but what we share —
For the gift without the giver is bare.*

James Russell Lowell

Today I let you make your own decisions. I cannot expect you to make intelligent, big decisions later in life if I make all of your decisions for you now. You need lots of practice. You need to make little decisions, live them out and see how they work for you. Wherever it is safe, I will let you make your own decisions — what you wear, what you do, when you are hungry, who you do and do not like to play with, how you like to work. All these decisions are a very important part of your getting to know who you are and how you interact with the world. I will not impose myself on you. I will give you a chance to get to know yourself.

**I allow you the privilege
of making your own decisions.**

Nature fits all her children with something to do.

James Russell Lowell

Today I will recognize your love as a gift in my life. Your love has always felt so good to me. It travels inside me like a healing balm or a peaceful summer rain. When I make mistakes, you forgive me so freely. Your love for me is unconditional. I see the love you feel for me in your eyes and your tender gestures. I will not take your love for granted nor assume that it is somehow owed me. I do not have a right to your love. It is a gift that you give me and I am deeply grateful for it. Your love humbles me — you seem to accept me for what I am even when I cannot do that for myself. I thank my Higher Power for allowing me this experience.

**Your love is a spiritual gift
and I am ever grateful to you for it.**

And yes I said yes I will yes.

James Joyce

I will let you push me away today and I will
not fall over. Beginning with crawling
away from me steadily on upward, you test
me and push me away. Today I understand
that you are not pushing me away so much
as experimenting with longer and longer dis-
tances for yourself. I see that it is vital that
I hold my place and act as a reference point
in your world that you can leave and return
to over and over again. If I tip over or disappear, your energy will have to go into finding me rather than into finding yourself, and
you will not be able to keep your mind
where it belongs — on your own life. Like a
parent at a large picnic, I will lay my blanket
out and stay there so you will know where
to find me when you need to check in or I
will tell you where I have gone so you will
not worry.

**I remain stable and steady
while you find your feet in the world.**

We must be our own before we can be another's.

Ralph Waldo Emerson

Today I will wait patiently for you. I will adjust my speed to your needs and I will find a cozy, warm spot inside myself and wait quietly. I will wait as you tell me fully what you need to say. I will not rush, inter-rupt or correct you. Instead of preoccupying myself with the next thing I have to do, I will focus on you. I will hear not just your words but feel your desire to communicate. I will be open to taking you into myself. I will receive you with communion, prayer and gratitude in my heart. Today it pleases me just to be near you.

**Your words fall on my ears
like a caressing warm spring breeze.**

you are my sun, my moon and all my stars

e e cummings

Today I amuse myself with pleasant thoughts of you. I remember you as the tender baby in my arms who felt so full and alive. I see you in my mind's eye in toddlerhood reaching out a chubby arm, knees and back slightly bent, face full of wonder. You in your first years of school struggling to read — so thrilled to decode the world of letters. You experimenting with older roles, trying words and attitudes on for size, shuffling them around to form a personality. You growing into the mature and wonderful person you are today. I am so grateful and proud to know you and to have you in my life.

**You are a deep source of
pride and joy in my life. I thank you.**

*In people's eyes, in the swing . . . in the triumph
and the jingle and the strange high singing of some
aeroplane overhead was what she loved; life; London; this moment in June.*

Virginia Woolf

Today I feel all of my own feelings and do not ask you to feel them for me. Sometimes, for instance, when I deny my own anger, eventually we have some interaction and you end up angry. Today I notice that I participate in provoking that at times because when you express anger it relieves me of some of my own. I understand in recovery that this is not fair or healthy. I know that I need to take responsibility for all of my feelings and feel them myself. It is only then that I can allow you to feel freely and express your own feelings without being threatened by confusing them with mine. You cannot hope to separate from me if I cannot first separate from you.

**I am responsible for my
feelings and you are responsible
for yours.**

Freedom is possibility . . .

Soren Kierkegaard

What does it mean today to love my child? One more small act of caring. One extra moment of my time. A soft response even though I am tired. Greeting her warmly. Asking her how she is and listening to her response with concerned attention. If I say that I love my daughter today, let me show it. Words without accompanying actions are empty and make children become mistrustful and disheartened. If I love my child I must show her that I love her by the way I treat her. Today I will demonstrate my love.

I love my child and I can show it.

Words fly up, thoughts remain below.
Words without thoughts, never to heaven go.

William Shakespeare

Today I will let things be — simple words of wisdom: "Let It Be." I forget this so often — to relax and let it be. There is such wisdom in these words. In them lie all the lessons of trust, faith, respect, non-harming and peace. What we can let be will let us be. This is not a passive but a highly motivated spiritual act. It is a recognition of our surrender to a Higher Power and our willingness to be fully engaged in life. Only a person who is truly connected can let it be because it is an act of faith and courage and strength.

I will live life today and let it be.

A man is rich in proportion to the number of things which he can afford to let alone.

Henry David Thoreau

Today I will give my child the greatest gift a parent can give — my time. Today when my child speaks to me, I will listen. I will look at his face and see his heart. I will feel his earnest desire to communicate with me and I will love him for it. I will get less done today and spend more time just being with my child, knowing that my presence now while I have him near me will be carried with him inside his heart. The attention I give him freely today will be the attention he will freely give himself tomorrow.

**Today I treasure my moments
with you; knowing that they
are numbered makes them
more precious.**

I throw myself down in my chamber, and I call and invite God and his angels thither, and when they are there, I neglect God and his angels, for the noise of a fly, for the rattling of a coach, for the whining of a door.

John Donne

Today I will allow my children to position themselves where they need and choose to be. I will trust their instincts as being right for them. I will not tell them who they are. I will hold out a space in the world where they can be. I will carve out room for their truth and defend it. I will honor their right to be. I will be strong for them. They have a right to look to me for love and nurturance. I brought them into this world and it is up to me to provide a safe place for them in which to grow. Watching them become fully expressive, happy people is its own reward.

I create a safe place for my children.

Give me where to stand, and I will move the earth.

Archimedes

Today I will share my child with the world. I will not attempt to hang on to my child or feel that I am the only person who could possibly understand her. Today I know that other people have a great deal to give her and I will not interfere with what others wish to share with her. Each moment I let go a little more as I watch my child take energetic steps into the world that awaits her. I will have confidence in her and her ability to make good connections for herself that have nothing to do with me.

**My child belongs to herself
and to the world; I am her nurturer;
she has her own Higher Power.**

Iron rusts from disuse; stagnant water loses its purity and in cold weather becomes frozen; even so does inaction sap the vigor of the mind.

Leonardo da Vinci

Today I will let my child separate from me, knowing that it is part of the important work she has to do in life. I am responsible for her in childhood, but some day she will have to be responsible for herself and take care of herself in a world beyond me. Just as a bird needs to leave the nest to learn to fly, my child needs to leave the nest to learn to be her own person. This is not a rejection of me but an affirmation of herself, and if she is willing and able to separate from me, I will know that I have done my job as parent well; that I have nurtured and loved her and allowed her to find the strength within herself to do this awesome thing called living life.

**Today you are free, my sweet,
to live your life; my love and blessings
go with you on your journey.**

I want this to be yours in the sense that if you find it and read it, it will be there in you already and the leaflet then merely something to leave behind.

Adrienne Rich

Today I will take care of my own needs and not meet them through my children. I will find sources of nourishment and acceptance from others in my life; I will not place that burden only upon my children's shoulders. I will accept the love that they bring to me gratefully as a gift from a Higher Source but I will not demand their love. I will be touched by their acceptance of me as I am but I will not cling to it and make it more important than my own acceptance of myself. I will not feed off their spirit but will develop and nurture my own. Their spirit belongs to them, mine to me, and we can make music together if we each have an instrument of our own to play.

**Today I know that as parent
it is my role to take care of my children,
not theirs to take care of me.**

Seek not, my soul, the life of the immortals; but enjoy to the full the resources that are within thy reach.

Pindar

I will be brave today. I am faced with a job that feels awesome and enormous, for which I sometimes feel ill-equipped. I will face these challenges with a strong heart. Where I feel I do not know enough, I will read and find sources of information within my community to expand my knowledge. Where I feel inadequate to the vital job of child-rearing, I will share my insecurities openly and humbly with someone who will understand what I am talking about and offer me support. I do not have to know everything before I start. I can learn along the way if I am sincere in my desire to do the best job I am capable of doing.

I humbly seek help and guidance as I need it, knowing that this is too big a job for me to try to do all alone.

Life well spent is long.

Leonardo da Vinci

Today I will recognize a special quality that my child possesses. Each of us has gifts to give and today I will identify one of my child's. I will point it out to him and nurture it. I will help him to recognize this in himself as being of true value to himself and those around him. Today I understand that each person on this earth has his own gifts, qualities that they did not work for but which just seem to be a natural part of who they are. Qualities I tend to take for granted or even discount. Today I will see them for the gifts that they are, draw them out and bring them fully to light.

**I recognize the unique gifts
that you bring to life and I celebrate
them in you.**

All we know is still infinitely less than all that remains unknown.

William Harvey

*T*oday I will not get in your way. I know that when I am hurried or impatient, I do for you what you can easily do for yourself and thus remove from you the experience of being self-sufficient. Each time you are able to take care of yourself successfully, your self-esteem increases, your sense of accomplishment is palpable. Today I will wait while you learn a lesson for yourself that I could have taught you in a minute, understanding that if the readiness is not there within you, my words are meaningless. I will create a safe environment in which you may learn for yourself. When you have done that, I will congratulate you on your accomplishment and in no way minimize its importance to you or take it away from you for my own self-gratification.

**I see you as an explorer
in life and I assist you
in your journey.**

Personal space refers to an area with invisible boundaries surrounding a person's body into which intruders may not come.

Robert Sommer

Today I enter the present moment with you. Often I dwell in the past or in the future but today I understand that all we really have is today. If I live this moment fully appreciating all of the wonder and beauty that is present in it, tomorrow really will take care of itself. If I throw away today, I may be tempted to do the same with tomorrow. But if I appreciate and take in the good that it can give me, tomorrow will have a better chance. I will share today with you, knowing that it will never appear in either of our lives quite in this way again.

**I welcome the moment and
the richness that lies within it.**

Look to today for it is life — the very life of life.

Sanskrit poem

Today I will take as good care of myself as I do of those around me. I will listen to the voice of the child inside of me and respond with kindness and understanding. If I am tired, I will find a way to rest. If I am anxious, I will create some quiet time and let go of my anxiety in meditation. If I am hungry, I will enjoy eating. If I do not take care of myself, I will be running on empty, and resentment and anger will build in me toward those I am taking care of. I cannot give away what I don't have within me, so I will nurture within myself what I would like to give to my children. I will do what it takes to take care of myself.

**I pay attention to my own needs today.
It is okay to have them.**

No man is an island entire of itself; every man is a piece of the continent, a part of the main.

John Donne

Today I remember that the job of parenting is long-term and I will keep the overall picture in my mind. I naturally have goals in my job of parenting. If I do not reach them as quickly as I might like to, I will remember that people are "works in progress." We are not meant to be nicely packaged. We are human and we are supposed to live and learn. Sometimes I tighten up inside and get anxious and frustrated because things are not just where I want them to be. But on the other hand, why should they be? Life is a process, parenting is a process and real wisdom lies in enjoying the journey — there really is no finish line.

**Today I enjoy the process of
parenting and understand that
life takes time.**

*Accept the place the divine providence has found for
you, the society of your contemporaries, the connection of events.*

Ralph Waldo Emerson

Today I remember the day you were born and what I felt. The tender beauty of your face, your tiny hands and feet so perfect and so small; the way it felt to hold you in my arms, such a sense of quiet magnificence all wrapped up in you. How with awe and gratitude I watched breath enter and leave your body and I understood something about the progression of man and God and my own parents. Could I have been loved like this too perhaps? Today I remember how when I held you, nothing else seemed quite as important anymore. I recall the silent promises that poured from my heart onto you and the love I felt that seemed almost to belong to another dimension it was so sweet.

**Today I am deeply grateful
just for your life — just your being here
is all it takes for me to love you.**

*Deep within the starry night
Comes she through with steady flight
Upon the sea upon the air
She rides with stardust in her hair.*

T.D.

Today I regard my children as the teachers of my spirit. My love for them and my desire to do right by them, not to fail them, make me willing to examine myself in a way I might not otherwise do. I would rather look into my heart and prove myself wrong through my own investigation than be right at their expense. If I can come through this experience of parenting knowing that I have given it my absolute best shot, then I will sleep at night. Today I have the opportunity to do the best I can do — that is, give all I have to give. If I give them who I am, perhaps they can forgive me for what I am not.

I give my children the best of me.

The life of the law has not been logic, it has been experience.

Oliver Wendell Holmes, Jr.

*T*oday I do and release, I perform an action and let go of the fruits. If each time I do something I second-guess myself, I will drive myself and those around me crazy. I cannot control everything. If I send my child on his way and then proceed to worry about him all day, I am robbing each of us — I am robbing myself of my own time and him of a parent who has confidence in him and can separate. I am capable of performing my actions and letting go of the results. In this I gain great freedom because I am no longer tied up in control and worry. I leave a little space for the Higher Power to work.

I let go of results.

Once a decision was made, I did not worry about it afterward.

Harry S Truman

I felt a part of my family in my very soul and wanted the world to know who we all were. I thought the rhythm of my family was the rhythm of the world. My parents were archetypes to my young mind, representing man and woman. My brothers and sisters were like demi-gods and goddesses to me. I tried to pattern myself after them. The loss of my family was the loss of me — the destruction of a childhood truth and the mythology of my life. It was because I had a family that it hurt so deeply to lose it. No matter how disease destroyed my family — I did have one and I love them.

I honor and feel the love I had for my family.

In that brief hour I saw a family business that would rival any other. I pictured this struggling town experiencing a financial rebirth; people from all over driving to see us. Here was an idea that would allow us to work together, celebrate our past and share it with the world.

Peter Hedges

110

Today I will have faith in my child's autonomy. I have taken care of him for so long, met his physical needs, organized his life and dealt with his problems that I have a hard time feeling that he can get along without me occasionally. It is such a valuable lesson for a child to know that he can function happily, separate from his parents; that he will not fall apart if his parents aren't there to hold him together. Even though I know this intellectually, my instinctual self wants to overprotect my child and have him near me. It will also be good for him to learn that he is safe apart from me.

**I envision safety and happiness
for you on your own.**

Finish each day and be done with it . . . You have done what you could; some blunders and absurdities no doubt creep in; forget them as soon as you can. Tomorrow is a new day; you shall begin it well and serenely.

                                   Ralph Waldo Emerson

Today I will say less and do more. I know that children become what they behold. The greatest teaching I give my children is not what I say but who I am. Today I will be what I tell them they should be and first see within myself if it is possible. If I cannot live up to what I ask my children to be, I have no right to demand it of them. The greatest impact we have on our children is what we model. If we are confident and strong, they will internalize our confidence and strength as a part of them. If we are resentful underneath, they will take that in as a part of themselves. If we are loving toward ourselves and others, they will receive that within them.

**Today I will be what I wish
for my children.**

The only true amends is a change in behavior.

Sharon Wegscheider-Cruse

Today I will pay attention to the contents of my child's dreams. When he says to me, "I had a dream last night," I will really listen to what it was about, knowing that it has significance. Sometimes we do not let ourselves know what is going on with us underneath. Dreams can help us to see what we might have ignored by daylight. They are messages to our conscious minds and good to listen to. I will let myself muse over the meaning of my own dreams and take interest in those of my child's. They might have something to tell me. In any case they are interesting and fun.

**I will search within myself
and my child for depth and meaning.**

The whole creation is essentially subjective, and the dream is the theater where the dreamer is at once scene, actor, prompter, stage manager, author, audience and critic.

Carl Jung

Today I will waste some time with myself and my child. Sometimes I forget that wasting time together can have a virtue all its own. I once had a friend refer to "important hang-out time" spent as children: time of small exchanges, creating little amusements, time of cementing relationships and building trust. The hours we fritter away together with our children, doing nothing in particular, are some of the most enjoyable and life is meant to be enjoyed. Sometimes our business gets in the way of living. We have the illusion of going toward something of consequence when really we are going away from something much more important.

I will ease up and waste time with my child today.

It is the time I wasted for my rose that makes her so important.

Antoine de St. Exupery

Today I will keep the focus on myself.
Whenever I feel my mind wave around
in search of another mind to enter, I will
bring myself back. My mind is a very fluid
thing. It can easily leave my body and life
experience and go in search of another. But
what's the point? Then it won't be here to
direct my own day and when it returns, it
will be in an agitated, irritable state because
its wandering activity makes it off center.
Today I will choose activities that nourish
my mind rather than drain it. I will explore
relaxation, meditation, spiritual reading and
prayer. If my mind is mine to use as I
choose, then I will choose wisely.

I grow by myself and share from here.

*For my thoughts are not your thoughts, neither are
your ways my ways.*

The Bible

Today when I feel my buttons pushing me to the point of great pain, I will see it as an opportunity for growth. Life is constantly offering me situations that help me to come in touch with my deep fears. Today I understand that this is how I grow. If I keep running away from these situations, blaming them on the other party, I will only cheat myself. I need to ask myself what is it in me that is so anxious. What am I afraid of? I have a wonderful gift for self-diagnosis if I allow myself to look. No one knows me as well as I. Today I will not avoid — I will look and ask myself the important questions.

I turn my gaze inward today.

For fools rush in where angels fear to tread.
But where's the man whose council can bestow,
Still pleased to teach, and yet not proud to know.

Alexander Pope

*T*oday I am breaking the chain of generational addiction in my family. I am feeling my pain and dealing with it, rather than passing it down to my children in the form of unreasonable expectations and rules. If I can break this chain in my lifetime, I will have passed freedom of choice on to my children and grandchildren. If this is all that I ever accomplish in my lifetime, my existence would be completely worthwhile. What I am giving as an inheritance is that which is truly worthwhile — the right to search out their own truth. Today I choose life for myself and my progeny.

**I love and bless this
beautiful path of spiritual recovery.**

Human reason needs only to will more strongly than fate, and she is fate.

Thomas Mann

I will hold my temper today. I will not let little things throw me off balance, and if I feel my temperature rising, I will pause, breathe deeply a few times and remember my desire to remain calm. When I lose my temper with my children, they never really learn anything from it except to be afraid. Today I understand the difference between setting a reasonable rule with consequences that I am willing to follow through on when it is not respected, and shouting out a rule in a moment of unbridled anger. That rule is not born out of care and negotiation; it is a dictum spoken in heat and teaches only negative lessons. I am in better command of myself today.

**Today I accept anger as
a natural feeling and I choose
appropriate ways to let it out.**

Anger raiseth invention, but it overheateth the oven.

George Savile, Marquess of Halifax

Today I have more than packaged humility. I do not merely espouse words that sound humble while underneath I hide my arrogance. In recovery it is more important to me to be real than to look good. Being real shows in my willingness to live in acceptance of who I am today without trying to look and sound superior to those around me. I will not rob my humanity and peace of mind from myself today by pretending to be something I am not. I will also not be arrogant about personal growth, holding my new learning over my children and other people. What I hold over others' heads, I have not truly integrated into myself. I am who I am. I am doing the best that I can and that is enough for me today.

**It is okay just to be as
far along in life as I truly am.**

Humility is to make a right estimate of one's self.

Charles Hadden Spurgeon

*T*oday I take a proactive position rather than a reactive one. I will move into my life with courage. I will act on my day and not wait for my day to act on me. I will support my children in seeing themselves as people with choices, and when they bring me their concerns, I will sit down with them and focus on solutions. I will listen to all that they tell me. Then I will search out choices with them for handling the situation. There is enough room in life for all of us to come out winners. We can support each other in our positive decisions and directions for ourselves. I am not a victim and my children are not victims. We are active choice-makers with bright futures.

**I take charge of my own life
and allow my child to take
charge of hers.**

*For hatred does not cease by hatred at any time:
hatred ceases by love — this is the eternal law.*

The Pali Canon

*T*oday if I am consistently experiencing discomfort with my child, instead of looking for its reasons in her life, I will try to remember what was going on for me when I was her age. Chances are that if I am stuck with her, I may have been stuck with myself around that age. My inability to locate and feel my own pain may be creating an emotional block in relation to my child. It is not easy to go back to my own childhood at my age to better understand my present, but I owe it to myself and my child to give it a try. Once I get in touch with what is going on for me, I may experience a shift in perception that will allow light to shine through the cracks. There is great hope and relief in owning my truth and today I am willing to search it out.

Today I will examine my own life first — then my child's.

Emotion is the chief source of all becoming conscious. There can be no transforming of darkness into light and of apathy into movement without emotion.

Carl Jung

Today I will stay with my own life and resist the temptation to get lost in other people's. My desire to think more about other people's lives than my own only says something about me. Even if I don't like someone's behavior, crossing over the line into obsessing about them is still not wise or justifiable. Any time my energy is being drained through my constant preoccupation with someone else's life, I need to ask myself why I am doing that. The answer might be a habit from childhood or fear of betrayal, but what I need to remember is that betrayal is part of the disease, so to fear betrayal from a person with this disease is to fear getting wet in a rainstorm. I need to provide myself with an umbrella or stay inside.

**I am fed and nourished from
the center within me.**

If fifty million people say a foolish thing, it is still a foolish thing.

Anatole France

122

Today I remember that I am on a spiritual path of recovery. I know that as I internalized who my parents were, so will my child internalize who I am. I am grateful that recovery has come my way and that I have this opportunity to improve my own life and the life of my child by simply *being different*. Internal change is a mysterious thing. It is a true reworking of the past and takes a great deal of courage. Essentially life must be lived in the present, but for this to be possible our past needs to be resolved so that it does not impact the present in harmful ways.

I understand how to rework my past.

I am a camera with its shutter open, quite passive, recording, not thinking. Recording the man shaving at the window opposite and the woman in the kimono washing her hair. Some day, all this will have to be developed, carefully printed, fixed.

Christopher William Bradshaw

I can make plans today. When I was young I could not count on plans being honored. I would get very excited about something and then it would mysteriously fall through. My parents would forget to pick me up on time or would not remember that I had something important to do. I felt forgotten about and hurt. As a defense against feeling more pain, I stopped making plans for myself and pretended that having things happen as I hoped they would didn't matter to me. It hurt to lose my courage to dream, but not as much as being quietly wounded over and over and over again. When I make myself a promise, I take it seriously and I do the same for my children.

I can think, hope and dream again.

You analyze their dreams . . . I give them the courage to dream again.

Jacob L. Moreno

Today I will be strong. I will not let someone else's shortcomings be an excuse for me to fall apart. I have strength within me if I use it. I cannot control anyone's behavior but my own. If I am sincere in my path for personal growth, I will understand that the relationship I need to work out first is the relationship with myself. When I look into the mirror, I need to feel good about who I see there. I am entitled to like myself and do what it takes to bring that about. If I like myself, my children will feel permitted to like themselves too. Maybe that's the way it's meant to be.

I will reach inside for strength.

The good befriend themselves.

Sophocles

I will not blame myself today for what I feel might be your shortcomings. Even if things I have done might have contributed, I know that all along I have been doing my best, and what I did not know yesterday I did not know. I let go of yesterday and forgive myself today so that I can move on. Only this way can I bring my best self to you. Once I am aware of any wrongdoing on my side, I will make sincere and full amends. I will forgive myself and ask your forgiveness. Then I will change my behavior remembering that amends without a change in behavior are not true amends.

**I let go of self-blame and
forgive myself fully and freely.**

Conscience is the perfect interpreter of life.

Karl Barth

Today I allow my present to work out. Sometimes the idea of a peaceful, fulfilling life seems like a leap into a dangerous unknown. The changeability and mood swings of my family taught me to mistrust calm. I almost felt relief when the top would blow off in the family because it was better than waiting for it to. I lived with the constant awareness that the good times wouldn't last and now it's a very hard habit to break. I keep waiting for things to fall apart. Can it really be this good? Can life be easy with occasional crises? My past taught me that life was a crisis with occasional respites. Today I see that I need to learn a new way of living. It may feel strange but I will keep at it.

I am willing to try.

Wait for the wisest of all counselors, Time . . .

Pericles

Today I will not disappear into my feelings and be unavailable to my child. My parents were often preoccupied with what was going on inside them and I could not reach them. I find that I do that too and I fear that my children cannot reach me. When I am afraid or hurt, I get lost in the feelings triggered from my past and find it difficult to make my way back to the present. It is a double pain — one is the pain of being lost to myself and the other is the pain of being lost to my children because I know how it feels to them. Today I have tools that I can use. When I need help, I can reach out and get it. I don't have to stay stuck in my past anymore; I can find my way back.

I will work through my feelings.

Life consists of what a man is thinking of all day.

Ralph Waldo Emerson

Today my goals will be realistic for my family. We do not need to look like the Donna Reed Show for me to feel that we are happy. We can be a "good enough" family — a family in which needs are met, not necessarily brilliantly but well enough, so that our children can move on to their next stage of development without being held back and we can all feel secure and continue to grow. If in reaction to my own painful past I attempt to make my family perfect, I will only hurt them in a different way. No one is on top of the world all the time and I want to give my children the comfort of knowing that. They don't have to be constantly terrific to alleviate my anxiety. Today my kids can be real.

I allow my children to go up and down in their development.

Life is like playing a violin in public and learning the instrument as one goes on.

Samuel Butler

Today I allow my children to have mood swings without my mood altering along with theirs. The mood swings that I experienced in my home as a child were terrifying to me and left a deep mark on my psyche. I am constantly scanning other people and their moods, waiting for them to swing. Because of my own emotional setup, when my children's moods swing, which is a natural part of childhood, I over-react. I either do anything to pacify them or I show no patience and try to get them to shut down as fast as I can. Changeability in children is natural. Oftentimes it is related to their hormones and they really can't do a lot about it. My reaction may have more to do with fear from my past than with what is going on in the present.

**I separate my child
from my own past struggles.**

Integrity simply means a willingness not to violate one's identity.

Erich Fromm

I will give you time to grow, knowing that you are a work in progress. You are not the end result of anything but each day a new constellation of beginnings. I will not rush you. Anything worth doing is worth doing well; I will let you take your full complement of hours in growing up. Each lily on the surface of the water has roots that reach deep into the lake. Each thought or action on your surface has roots deep in your subconscious. Today I will respect the root system that you are taking time to build.

You may take the time you need to grow up.

The imagination of a boy is healthy, and the mature imagination of a man is healthy; but there is a space of life between in which the soul is in a ferment, the character undecided, the way of life uncertain.

John Keats

I can forgive myself today. For some reason I would rather forgive anyone else but myself. I can't understand why. Perhaps if I forgive myself I really have a chance at that happiness I am always talking about. Maybe that just seems scary. Maybe it means I'll have it and lose it again and that seems like too much to bear. But if the truth were to be told, life is always having and losing, and if I have survived it this far, I can dare again. I will forgive myself at a deep level for what I feel I no longer want to carry. I will let my family forgive me without resisting them. I am ready to give and receive love.

I forgive myself fully and completely.

There is no witness so dreadful, no accuser so terrible as the conscience that dwells in the heart of every man.

Polybius

*T*oday I recognize my part in a painful interaction. My part is the only one I can do anything about. I no longer need to convince myself that someone else is in the wrong. The truth always lies in between. Sometimes I focus on the other person because secretly I blame myself for everything. I no longer need to do that; that is a position from childhood. Today I know that I wasn't to blame then and I am not to blame now. If I have made a mistake, I will try to set things right. If another person will not let me do that, I cannot do more; if I try to, then that is dysfunction. If something is not working, I need to let it go and move on. It might change later.

I let go of my own dysfunctional reaction.

A prudent mind can see room for misgiving, lest he who prospers should one day suffer reverse.

Sophocles

Today I see that reparenting my own wounded child is absolutely necessary if I am to parent my own children with freedom and clarity. Bringing up my children puts me in touch with my own inner child as nothing else could. Today I see this as nature's way to give myself a second chance. When my own issues are kicked up by what my child is experiencing, I will go directly to the source and ask myself what was going on for me in my own childhood that makes it so painful for me to see what is happening with my child. Through my love for my child I have an opportunity to re-feel my own past and let it go. This way we will both grow and change.

I will reparent myself.

When one door closes, fortune will usually open another.

Fernando de Rojas

Today I grant myself and my family their liberty. Somehow the commitments of family life get mixed up in my mind with control and power. It is hard just to be in my family and grant freedom to all of us within it. I begin to believe in the illusion of control and trying to control things becomes a habit. When I do this I miss the forest for the trees. I organize the events but forget how to participate in them and enjoy them. In my role as parent I do need to organize, but after that I want to learn to step back and be a part of things in an easy natural way. Controlling my children is not healthy for them or me. In granting them personal freedom I can give it to myself as well.

**I give freedom to myself and
my family members.**

The love of liberty is the love of others. The love of power is the love of ourselves.

William Hazlitt

Today I will come closer to my own truth. I cannot hope to allow my children their own truths if I do not understand my own. A friend once told me that if he wanted a beautiful suit, he went to a tailor so that he could choose the fabric and have the suit made to fit his particular form. He felt the same about his life — that it should be tailored to suit his particular needs and desires. When I love someone else's life, I am always vaguely uncomfortable. I do better when I pay attention to my own personality traits and allow myself the freedom to pursue my likes and avoid my dislikes. I will tailor my life to suit me and teach my children how to do that for themselves.

**I let myself be who I am
and my children be who they are.**

To be an individual one must be a non-conformist.

Ralph Waldo Emerson

Today I will thank my children for the little things they do for me. Sometimes I get so stuck in the gear of taking care of them that I don't see the many ways in which they try to take care of me. There is so much love in their gestures and it is so very important to them that I show them how much I appreciate what they do. If I want them to grow up to be giving people, I need to show them that it is worth it to give; that what they give will be seen and appreciated. It is also good for me to remember that receiving is the other side of giving and equally important. If we cannot receive gratefully, then life cannot give us anything.

I receive with an open grateful heart.

The sight of you is good for sore eyes.

Jonathan Swift

We have different feelings — you and I. We do not see anything in exactly the same way; nor should we. To attempt to create this state would be to live in co-dependency. We each have a right to our own feelings. We can speak those feelings without making them match up with each other's in order to feel safe. It is okay for us to feel different things at the same time — that is normal and healthy. It is not necessary that I agree with what you tell me, but it is necessary that I help you to feel heard. The same goes with me — you do not have to agree with all that I say; just hear me out.

I am me, you are you.

Innocence has nothing to dread.

Jean Racine

Today I will not live on the edge of my chair. I will not expect the worst. In the past part of my modus operandi was to anticipate anything that might go wrong in advance. Today that attitude produces uncertainty and insecurity in my relationship with my child. In fact real crises are few and far between. I need not live as if they were happening daily any more; that level of chaos belongs to my past. In normal living crisis is the exception and not the rule, and if I live as if crisis were always around the corner, I run the risk of creating trouble where it doesn't need to exist. It is so important for the peace of my family that I let go of these old habit patterns.

I release my old crisis mentality.

Faith, sir, we are here today and gone tomorrow.

Aphra Behn

Today I will share something of my cultural tradition with my children. Each of us comes from somewhere and that somewhere we come from is part of what forms our culture. Even if my background is not lustrous in any way, it is part of who I am, and who I am is all that I have to give my child. My child loves hearing stories about me when I was young; it is meaningful to him in ways I can't even imagine and it creates an intimate sharing between us. I still remember the stories that my parents shared with me about their childhoods. They created mental pictures. These are all a part of the cultural tradition I share with my child.

**I share spoken memories
with my child.**

Eternity was in that moment

William Congreve

Today I will build on the positive strengths from my past. I will continue to release pain, anger and resentment in whatever way works for me and then I will allow happy times and feelings to surface in my mind. When they do, I will fully feel and enjoy the memory and re-experience the joy, confidence and sense of well-being they produced in me. These feelings are extremely important to my recovery of a full and happy self. These are feelings about myself that I pass on to my children. My children take in at a deep level how I feel about myself and they model those feelings. I want them to see me demonstrate actively the strength and joy that I bring with me from my youth.

**I see the beauty and love
that was mine.**

We have just enough religion to make us hate, but not enough to make us love one another.

Jonathan Swift

Today I will trust your own soul to light your way and mine to light mine. Within you lies all you need to know. There is a light that shines for you — a God center in your heart that is the seat of your growth and development. I am here to support you and love you in your journey, not to divine what that journey is. You belong to a world beyond me and you arrive specially suited to be a member of it. There is a spiritual light within you and that is the source that will always be yours and on which you can depend. For this brief time that we have together, I will share my light with you, but never so much that it overshadows yours. Let the light within me be a mirror for you of the light within you and visa versa.

I see the light that shines within you.

Be lamps unto yourselves. Be a refuge unto yourselves. Do not turn to any external refuge.

The Pali Canon

I can try a different approach today. Just because I did things one way yesterday does not mean that I have to do them the same way today. I am not tied to my past actions. My children are so wonderful to practice this with because they are constantly changing and experimenting with new things themselves. They are always willing to try something new. When I try a new idea with them, they respond so quickly. Because they are young, I have a real opportunity to correct past errors by changing my approach today. Children heal and adjust miraculously fast, so now is the time to make changes and grow. Corrections can be made more quickly and easily in youth before habits are ingrained.

I will try a new approach today.

The life which is unexamined is not worth living.

Plato

Today I will speak words of love to you. I will let you know what love for you lives within my heart. I will not withhold or save for another day or a better moment the revealing of my feelings. How do I know that moment will ever come? What am I saving up for? What strange philosophy of moderation keeps me from speaking to you fully and freely of my deep and passionate love for you? You are the one thing in my life that puts all the rest of my life into a different place, another perspective, and yet I forget to tell you how important you are to me. Heart of my heart, today I will tell you how much I love you.

I open my heart and mouth to you.

A great ox stands on my tongue.

Aeschylus

Today I know that there is much that I cannot see and I trust that it lies quietly in wait. I am tilling a plot that will grow and bear fruit. Each caring act I perform toward you nurtures the soil of your inner garden. Even if I do not know what is to come, I understand that what I do today is inextricably connected to tomorrow. The seeds I sow today will bloom in springtime and the extra care I take will be worth it. Some days you don't seem at all to be what you will become. Raising children can be confusing. I need to remember all that lies unseen in various stages of formation and growth.

I take a deeper look today.

In our springtime every day has its hidden growth in the mind, as it has in the earth when the little folded blades are getting ready to pierce the ground.

George Eliot

I will take joy in my children today. Children are here to remind us all of who we really are deep down. Situations that seem ordinary to me fill my child with wonder and excitement. Today I will recognize that he has the right idea — that life is meant to be felt and lived, that just being alive is enough. There is magic in the moment if I can find that place within me that recognizes it. Today I will find the child within me and join with my own child in a truer understanding of the meaning of life.

There is joy in both of our hearts today and when we share that joy, it grows.

Creatures of a day, what is man? What is he not? Mankind is a dream of a shadow. But when a God-given brightness comes, a radiant light rests on men, and a gentle life . .

Pindar

Today I abandon my heart and mind to what is ordinary within me and within my relationship with you. I see this humdrum life as a symphony of the Gods, a dance of the heavens. There is a palpable rhythm to this life that we lead, an ease and a grace that comes with being a person upon the earth with senses alive and willing. Everywhere I am surrounded by heavenly beauty even in what is not apparently beautiful. Everyday life has an elegance all its own and all of life is simply composed of thousands of ordinary days. The greatest gift I can give you is that of treasuring the moment.

Today I am aware of the beauty in ordinary days.

Without recognizing the ordinariness of Heaven, it is impossible to be a superior man.

Confucius

I can say I am sorry today. I can admit to being wrong. In the past I feared being scapegoated if I admitted my errors, but today I trust myself and my children to forgive and forget. When I can apologize to my child, we can move on. Neither of us has to react to the hurt surrounding an unresolved incident. I do not ask them to stuff feelings of resentment at being misunderstood or hurt. I also give my children permission to apologize to me by showing them that it is not so difficult and that it feels good. It is nice to clean house and release troublesome feelings.

I can say I am sorry.

Any man more right than his neighbors constitutes a majority of one.

Henry David Thoreau

Today I will fortify my child with love. The outside world can be rough and demanding. My job is to help my child to feel understood and valued so that when all is not perfect, she will have enough self-value to ride it out. I cannot tell her enough how terrific I think she is and how proud of her I feel. These messages will take hold at some level. I am her home where she comes for comfort, love and acceptance. I am not her school or her peer group. Let them do their work and I will do mine. My end of the bargain is to make sure that my child goes out into the world with my love in her heart.

I plant the seed of self-love within the garden in my child's heart.

Society attacks early when the individual is helpless.

B.F. Skinner

I will share a moment of joy with my child today. If there is an opportunity to feel something beautiful, I will find it. When I think back on my own childhood, I understand how valuable special moments were. I have remembered moments like that over and over and they have been a real source of strength and direction in my own life. Real joy is such a deep feeling. It connects me with my higher self. Children have the capacity to experience this feeling more than most people. Today I will join them in their joy and it will be a very special, precious communication between our two hearts.

I will carve out space to experience joy.

It is better that you should leave your work and sit at the gate of the temple and take alms of those who work with joy.

Kahlil Gibran

Today I will not drive myself so hard. I can't do everything; some things will have to wait and some will just not get done. That compulsion to keep moving and doing keeps me from what I really need to do — be with myself. It is hard to give things up and create a little space in my life. I so easily feel left out or envious of all that I think I am missing. I can live happily with the outside if I am in contact with the well of peace and tranquility within me. This is the message that I want my children to get from being with me — to value themselves and their home as I do.

**I take the time I need to be
whole and peaceful.**

The time to relax is when you don't have time for it.

Sydney J. Harris

Today I own my self. I cannot share a self with my children that I do not first have; I cannot give away what I do not own. If I don't work on building an inner self, I will live through my spouse, children, work or social position as if they were me and look to them to give me a self. This is a setup for co-dependency on both sides — a search for self in objects outside of the self; imbuing people, places and things with importance, meaning and power greater than my relationship with my self and my Higher Power. When I have a self safely built within me, I can share that with my family.

I will bloom where I am planted.

For a person to feel responsible for his actions, he must sense that the behavior has flowed from the self. It is easy to ignore responsibility when one is only an intermediate link in a chain of action.

Stanley Milgrom

Today I take responsibility for my anger and resentment. These feelings in me are most understandable given the circumstances of my past. I can allow the hurt and abandoned child within me to know that she has a right to these feelings and that they are true for her. She is not crazy, ungrateful, mean or bad. These feelings are to her credit; they mean that through it all she kept her soul alive and engaged. It is easy to slip into denial, to say that mature people can "put things aside," but if what you are putting aside is yourself, the price is too high. Anyway, there is no such thing as "putting aside" in this sense. One just finds another place to store or project these difficult feelings — into children, spouses, co-workers, etc. I might as well meet them head on.

I take myself seriously.

The way out is the way through.

Recovery Quote

Today I will not try to figure everything out but instead I will learn to live better with the question. I recognize that the deepest issues of life are a mystery and that to try to reduce life's issues to an easy formula will limit my experience. I understand that the mark of an educated person is not the amount of information he has managed to store but that he knows where to go to find it. The mark of a recovered person is not the "recovery" information he has accumulated and learned but his ability to live spontaneously and appropriately. My children come by spontaneity quite naturally. They become deeply involved in what they do, taking it very seriously then forgetting about it and moving on. When they are disturbed, they really feel upset, then it's over — all is forgiven. They seem content not to solve all of the world's problems every day.

I explore the question.

To have doubted one's own first principles is the mark of a civilized man.

Oliver Wendell Holmes, Jr.

Today I will take a different point of view. So much of life happens within my own mind. It is the minute-to-minute attitude that I take to every given moment. My attitude toward my children is so important. They pick up everything. How I see them influences how they see themselves. There is no reason for me to take a negative view of my child. If he is behaving in a way that is problematic, then he needs help. The assistance may be in the form of getting him help and/or getting help for myself. My issues have to be very clear before I can attribute my child's negative behavior entirely to him. Consciously or unconsciously I may be playing a part. I will give him a fresh start every day. He is free to grow and change.

I hold my child in a happy light.

To different minds, the same world is a hell and a heaven.

Ralph Waldo Emerson

*T*oday I know that God has a plan for me and that to know God is my highest goal. My children teach me spiritual lessons. My love for my children has given me a piece of heaven and the will to seek more. I am content with life because contentment is God's wish for me, my wish for my family and one of my spiritual values. I am not, however, complacent, smug or self-satisfied. There is always more to learn, explore and understand. Life is always there, waiting for me to tune in to it. This world vibrates; it is infused with vitality. It is there whenever I am ready to see it.

I reach for my Higher Power.

I just want to do God's will. And He's allowed me to go to the mountain. And I've looked over, and I've seen the promised land . . . So I'm happy tonight. I'm not worried about anything. I'm not fearing any man.

Martin Luther King, Jr.

Today I spurn the media's idea of success and I measure myself by my own yardstick. Everywhere I look, people seem to be younger, smarter and more fit than I am. There are four ways to relieve stress, three techniques for changing my life and five steps toward permanent success. This is not "one day at a time living." It is trying to swallow life whole — to gulp down experience. Today I understand that experience not only needs to be tasted and savored but also digested and assimilated. Too much of the best life has to offer leaves me exhausted. I will remember this when I schedule the lives of my children.

I find a sane and steady pace.

We are stardust.
We are golden,
And we've got to get ourselves
Back to the garden.

Joni Mitchell

Today I honor my struggle. That I have walked to the edge of madness in my alcoholic home and found my way back is why I am who I am. I understand the pain that feels as if it has no end, the confusion that makes common sense seem the possession of a privileged few. I understand being too ashamed to talk about these things because I am afraid of what people will think of me. I also know that there is poetry within my soul and music in my heart. When a day is gorgeous, I see that it is. I appreciate the little things. My complicated past has taught me much. It needn't be a burden I carry in silence; it can be a rich source of life and love and energy.

I am happy just for my life.

Madness need not be all breakdown. It may also be breakthrough. It is potential liberation and renewal as well as enslavement and existential death.

R. D. Laing

*T*oday I will forgive those in my past who have hurt me, like parents and siblings, because I have nothing better to do. If I wait for a good reason to forgive them, it may never come and I will carry this resentment and anger around forever. In the process of sweeping anger out the door, if a little resentment goes out with it, who will be the wiser? Why worry about giving them what I feel is the first break if it makes my heart lighter? It is the dynamic of the disease that I hate and why should I give the disease anything more of myself than it has already taken?

I forgive for my sake.

*Yes, you must leave everything that you cannot
    control,*
*It begins with your family, but soon it comes round
    to your soul.*
*I see where you're hanging, I think that I know how
    you're pinned,*
*If you're not feeling holy, your loneliness says that
    you've sinned.*

Leonard Cohen

*T*oday I recognize that how I say something carries as strong a message as what I say. If I have wonderful things to share but if the way I say them is hostile or cynical, people will naturally hear the anger and cynicism as loudly as the content, if not more. They will get a confusing double message and I will be frustrated because I will feel that no one wants to hear the good things I have to say. My delivery is a large part of my message and it will be heard for what it is. Often children understand subtext more accurately than text. They pick up tone, gesture, attitude and feeling clearly. If we then tell them only to hear our words and deny the truth of their effect, they will feel insecure if the two are at odds.

I will pay attention to the way I say things.

The medium is the message.

Marshall McLuhan

Today I rest quietly within the love I feel for my children. There have been few times in my life when I have loved like this. It recalls to me the way I felt about my parents as a very small child. My children are love teachers, they teach me to love. They teach me what it feels like to have my love for them be bigger than any other feeling in its way. This is one of God's ways of letting me glimpse true oneness and perfection. These are not ordinary feelings. They give me a place in the evolution of life. If I understand these feelings, they are a window into eternity. Any act performed with love is imbued with a power and presence that is of God. My children teach me to act in love.

I learn my lesson of love from my children.

If you have two loaves of bread, sell one and buy a hyacinth.

Persian Proverb

Today I will honor my feelings of resentment and anger from my past. I have no hope of ever working through them if I don't give some respect and space to the damaged child within me who went unprotected in an abusive situation. The fact that it was my family I loved and trusted more than any in the world, who shared in this situation is something I have had tremendous difficulty sorting out. Today I know that in order to get well I need to "accept the things I cannot change." Today I need to hold that child within me with all her fear and trembling and let her know that the adult me will not desert her. I can do for myself today what my family could not do for me then.

I parent my own inner child.

No man can lose what he never had.

Izaak Walton

*T*oday I recognize my tendency to presume that my child is feeling what I think he is feeling. Not only does this make him feel crowded out, but it is a way of denying to myself my own feelings about what I think he is feeling. This is the land of co-dependency where everybody is feeling everyone else's feelings and not feeling their own. If I can sort out which feelings are mine, then I can do something about them. I owe it to him and to myself to understand where I am coming from before I run headlong into his life situation. I will do a personal inventory first and then move from there.

I assess where I am coming from.

Learning from their children is the best opportunity most people have to assure a meaningful old age.

M. Scott Peck, M.D.

Today I speak from my heart. I don't have forever to be on this earth and if I waste my time, I will simply have wasted it. I do not mean that I should keep busy all of the time; only that while I am here, I will be true to my deeper truth and will share that part of myself with others. I will not take refuge in other people's ideologies and pretend that they are my truth; I will search out my own. Today I will not teach my children how to live farther away from their hearts, but I will let them teach me how to live closer to mine. I will be affected by them and let them affect me.

I see with my heart.

Who speaks the truth stabs falsehood in the heart.

James Russell Lowell

*T*oday I understand that my child needs encouragement — a little goes a long way. It's not easy to be young and she needs my love and support. It doesn't take much to think of a nice comment, a show of my confidence and good faith in her, and it means so much. There are also things that she doesn't need to hear — like unnecessary criticism. If I find fault in her too much, she will spend her life trying to figure out a way to please me and other authority figures in her life or she will tune out and put up a wall — both a setup for co-dependency. When she feels insecure, it will help her a lot if she feels that I think she is up to the task.

I find words of encouragement for my child.

Think before you speak is criticism's motto; speak before you think creation's.

E.M. Forster

Today I will seed my child into the world. Little by little I will plant him into activities and situations he can handle and that slowly grow in complexity. I will not push him before he is ready nor will I ignore his point of readiness out of my own laziness or fear. All that my child learns while he is young will stay with him as a baseline of experience and knowledge upon which he can build. I will first make sure that his home-life is secure, then I will set about helping him to make friends with the world he lives in and learn to manage it.

I help my child know himself in the world.

Let no youth have any anxiety about the upshot for his education . . . If he keeps faithfully busy each hour of the working-day, he may safely leave the final result to itself.

William James

Today I understand that all things spring from love — that is the well-hidden secret, the true meaning of life. Love and heaven are one and the same. If I wish to understand what this world needs, I will love it first. If I want to know how to live my life, to begin with I will love my life. If I want to understand my children, I will love them. It is through love that knowing and understanding come. I will choose in life the work that I love, then I will do it well. All we are really meant to do is to learn to love; the rest we will know in time. All wisdom, beauty and brilliance are contained in this feeling of love; they are qualities that will eventually exhaust themselves.

Today I am a student of love.

Neither a lofty degree of intelligence nor imagination nor both together go to the making of genius. Love, love, love, that is the soul of genius.

Wolfgang Amadeus Mozart

Today I recognize the little child who lives within my spouse. I love and nurture the child in you. I respond to your playfulness and see that part of you as life-giving and important. I see your hurt and disillusionment and I will try to be tender with you when you are wounded. I see the child in you come out through your eyes more each day and I welcome that youngster into my arms. I will let the child in me out so that we can be together. I will share your joy and listen to your tears. When you act belligerent or defensive, I will try to see the child behind this pose who feels that there is nothing there for him and doesn't want to look vulnerable. I will love this part of you and let you see and love this part of me.

I see the child who lives inside of you.

The power of the visible is the invisible.

Marianne Moore

Today I will not control my children's lives. My children live in this world in their own bodies; they get hungry, tired and sick apart from me. They will succeed and fail on their own. I can raise them as well as I can but they are here to follow their own destiny. It is not easy to know that I am ultimately powerless and to live day to day with that sense of powerlessness. This is where there is nothing left but prayer and turning it over to a Higher Power. I can let go more easily if I turn my child over to a Higher Power in prayer and meditation.

I release you to your ultimate good and entrust you to a Higher Power.

That energy which makes a child hard to manage is the energy which afterwards makes him a manager of life.

Henry Ward Beecher

*T*oday I will seek to increase my skills of perception and discernment. I will quiet my mind and observe. I will take a scientific approach and collect my own impartial data. I will attempt to be neutral and let observations fall onto a clean page in my mind. Today I will open my senses, mind and heart to let things in so that I can get the whole picture. There is so much information I block but now I will attempt to let those defensive walls down and really see. I will look at my children and try to understand them, not so much as I might like to see them, but as they really are.

I open my eyes today.

Children are entitled to their otherness, as anyone is; and when we reach them, as we sometimes do, it is generally on a point of sheer delight, to us so astonishing, but to them so natural.

Alastair Reid

Today I will capture the moment. I will play with it, stretch it out, move more deeply into it, extend it and savor it. In my busy life my tendency is to cut things short and return to consequential activity. Today I know that few things are of greater consequence than my relationship with you. The time I spend freely on you now is your real money in the bank. It is what you will draw on later in life for strength, fortitude and joy. If I wish to set up a trust account for you that will benefit you all your life, let it be this one — my love for you deposited day by day in a safe and secure place in your heart.

Today I search out the beauty in the moment.

The highest point a man can attain is not knowledge, or virtue, or goodness, or victory, but something even greater, more heroic and more despairing: Sacred Awe!

Albert Einstein

I send straight messages today. I let the fog
lift from my own brain and when I speak,
I concentrate on saying only one thing. Children hear everything and I know that if I am
saying one thing and feeling another, they
will internalize both messages and feel inadequate. They will not know what to do with
all of this conflicting information. They will
think that they just can't get things straight
and feel anxious and guilty for misunderstanding. They will be torn between what
their parent is saying and what their gut and
intuition tells them they are feeling but not
admitting.

I send clear messages today.

Children need models rather than critics.

Joseph Joubert

*T*oday I will hear what my child is saying. When she speaks, I will listen. I don't need to fix anything or make all her anxieties go away. I will just listen without advice — just hear. When I was young, I felt as if I had lost my voice, as if I were walking through a dream talking to people but no one knew that I was there. I tried to scream but no sound came out. There was such a gulf between what was going on inside of me and what anyone around me could hear me say. If someone could have listened to me, that's all it would have taken. It really doesn't take much. Listening and acknowledging is enough. Today I can do that for my child.

I will listen to my child.

Perhaps a child who is fussed over gets a feeling of destiny, he thinks he is in the world for something important and it gives him drive and confidence.

Benjamin Spock, M.D.

Today I will take a risk and I will allow my child to take one. It is good for me to try something new. There is no reason that time has to settle on me like a case of the bends. I am going to stretch, to try something that feels a little funny. There is something that I would like to add to my repertoire of life activities. I'm not comfortable doing it but I'd like to be so I'll give it a try. I'll ask my child for encouragement and advice. Children try new things all the time — maybe they can give me some tips. Perhaps we can even try something new together — even just something seemingly little, like going out for dinner together. Today I'll try it.

I will try something new today.

Life's aspirations come in the guise of children.

Rabindranath Tagore

Today I am glad that I am who I am in the spectrum of things. I have a sense of being where I am supposed to be. The situations I have lived, the lessons I have learned, the people I know seem to me to be who I am meant to know and be with. I have so much growing room inside of me — so many places to go, areas to explore. There are many things in my life that I can create and the first thing I create is myself. Who I am is my project, the task nearest my soul. This is the example I want to set for my children — to learn to understand themselves and their lives as a connection to life and eternity and God.

I am exactly where I am supposed to be.

Keep a green tree in your heart and perhaps the singing bird will come.

Chinese proverb

Today I commit myself to recovery for my sake and the sake of my children. I may have the ability to enter into the blissful state of denial but my children are sitting ducks. What I repress and am not willing to acknowledge and feel is felt by them. The elephant in the living room can come in many forms when we deny the pain in our own past or present because we are afraid to "open up a can of worms." That very fear tells us we are living with that "can of worms" within us. If we are not willing to examine its contents, we will pass it on unconsciously to our children. If we lie in small ways to our children, they will "hear" the lie and "know" the truth. What our children need in order to feel free and whole is the truth.

I will be honest.

The gods visit the sins of the father upon the children.

Euripides

Today I will not compare my children with other people's children. I will measure growth according to where they are and not where someone else is. There is so much competition and comparing built into their lives that I want home to be where their place is assured no matter how they perform. Home is where their love does not have to be bought. It is a gift. Eventually I hope that my children will learn that there is a place within them where they have access to a higher reality. I hope they will learn that there is more to life than people, places and things, that there is a life of the spirit.

I make no comparisons.

Envy slays itself by its own arrows.

Anonymous

Today I know that I need not wait to resolve every issue in a relationship in
order to get along with someone. Part of
health is knowing what can and cannot be
resolved at any given moment while I still
enjoy life. I will only be able to work anything out to the extent that I currently understand it, so even "working out" will
change its meaning for me. There are two
sides to this coin. One is thinking that I have
to work on virtually every detail of my life;
the other is to be smug and feel that the way
I do things is the way everyone ought to do,
which is denial. Neither extreme represents
health nor leads to happiness.

I live life a day at a time.

God grant me the serenity,
To accept the things I cannot change,
Courage to change the things I can
And the wisdom to know the difference.

                                    Reinhold Niebuhr
                                    AA Prayer

*T*oday I no longer need to be bewildered by my past. I have enough of the pieces to complete the puzzle. I understand, and in understanding I feel a kind of freedom. Now it is up to me to untie myself from the parts of my past and identity that I am caught in and to value and enjoy what is good. I see now that my feelings of mistrust were there for a reason — to protect myself from what I could not handle. Now I see that through understanding I can trust myself and that is real protection. I don't need to keep going back to learn the same lesson over and over again. Nor do I need to recreate all of my past pain in order to feel comfortable letting it go. I can accept and mourn a loss and move on. What is over is over; I give myself the gift of today.

I set myself free.

It's this simple: if I never try anything, I never learn anything. If I never take a risk, I stay where I am.

Hugh Prather

Today I will not seek protection by losing myself in the lives of my children. That will place an unconscious burden on them and even though I never really ask them to protect me, they will get the message. My job is to teach them to protect themselves. When they are young, they will learn this through my protecting them, and as they get older, they will learn it through watching how I protect and take care of myself. If I use them as buffers or an arena in which to get lost, I will find neither myself nor them. If I tell them to stand on their own but don't show them how, they will not believe it is possible.

**My children learn who they are
by seeing who I am.**

Romance fails us and so do friendships, but the relationship of parent and child, less noisy than all others, remains indelible and indestructable, the strongest relationship on earth.

Theodor Reik

Today I will open my mind to the excitement of the day. I will move out of high gear. I will relax and let it happen. Although I have plans, I will not become my plans. I will breathe deeply and slow down, remembering that it is not my day, but *how* I experience my day, that is important. Now I am ready to actually be with my children. Experiencing their day is something they do naturally. Until they are adolescents and capable of abstract thought, it is almost against their nature to split their minds into plans. They tend to engage freely in the activities that surround them in the present moment. Maybe that's why they are so much fun to be with. Perhaps there is more to this moment than meets the eye.

I will bring my mind and myself to the moment.

What a wonderful life I've had! I only wish I'd realized it sooner.

Colette

Today I will allow my children to make their own discoveries, to plumb the depths of their own souls in search of their wholeness. They need to ask their own questions and seek their own answers. If I make them realize my dreams, they will never have the chance to dream their own. There are few feelings in this world as sublime as finding what you love to do and doing it. When we do what we are made to do, we experience a sense of inner connectedness — we synchronize with ourselves, we're lined up with our own energies. It's a quiet strength. I want to encourage my children to find themselves and discover who they are, what they like and dislike. I want them to understand their relationship to life from the inside out.

I allow my children to be themselves.

Follow your bliss.

Joseph Campbell

Today I understand that I can do nothing about anyone but myself. Not to get in my children's path and do my best to make things better (or maybe worse) is an act of will that I am often not able to exercise. If other people feel angry or sad or frustrated, I feel that I have to help them to feel better before I continue to feel good myself. I need to recognize that getting certain people to feel better can be a lifetime job. It's just not within my power to help others do what they need to do to be happy. Happiness comes from within, from a deep realization that it's a better way to live. It is up to each person to come to this in his or her own time. I have a right to be happy all on my own.

I can live with someone else being in a difficult place.

Most folks are just about as happy as they make up their minds to be.

Abraham Lincoln

*T*oday I will speak my truth and leave it there. What I have to say needs to be said to clear my own conscience — not to get a response from someone else. It is not another person's job to make me feel okay about myself or that I have the right to say what I need to say. That's my job. I get into trouble when I try to turn my phrases to produce particular responses — especially when I give not because I want to give a particular thing but because I want it back. If I want something, I need to ask for it. If I give something, it is for free. This is how I wish to interact with my family and friends. This is what I want my kids to see — someone who stands where they are standing and doesn't ask other people to prop her up. This leaves a nice clear field for my children to learn to play on.

I give freely and ask for what I need.

The truth is more important than facts.

Frank Lloyd Wright

*T*oday I remember that each new area of personal growth carries with it new responsibility. I am responsible for what I see and understand. It is not that I have to do something about it. When we are children, often we are taught not to know what we know — that what our hearts and guts tell us is true. I will not teach that to my children. I will allow them to know what they know inside of them. They can act upon what they feel to be true for them, even if that action is just sharing their truth with me, where it is safe, and letting it go.

I will not talk myself or my children out of our truths.

Man must cease attributing his problems to his environment, and learn again to exercise his will — his personal responsibility in the realm of faith and morals.

Albert Schweitzer

Today I recognize that the intensity of my feelings may be too much for my child. She experiences things in her own way at her own level. My reactions to her life situations often say more about me than about her. If I impose my reaction on hers, she will feel that I don't trust her and will begin to mistrust herself. I need to find a window to her insides and reinforce her there. That way she will internalize the reinforcement as her own and it will build strength within her. This is about being seen and understood, not analyzed.

I offer support, not judgment.

All hatred driven hence,
The soul recovers radical innocence
And learns at last that it is self-delighting
Self-appeasing, self-affrighting
And that its own sweet will is Heaven's will.

William Butler Yeats

When I first held you in my arms and saw you smile, I felt as if the whole world were singing a greeting to you. I felt wise and strong. I could have fought a lion off to keep you safe — safe for me, safe someday for yourself. You slid to the earth on a rainbow and landed in my arms. All of me says yes, yes to love, yes to life, yes to your entry into this world. I can hardly know the depth of my love for you because it goes as deep as I go. Each day I am grateful for your presence, each day I pray for your presence, each day I pray for your well-being, each day you are a gift.

You are life's proof of life.

My little cookies, my big-small girls (boy),
My little chips of DNA whirling forward through the universe.
My double darlings, my double dollop of chocolate chip ice cream,
My little puppybody, my bubblegum reebok babies with the double dirty smile.

Erica Jong

Today I will not let my insecurities rule the way I perceive what is going on in my child's life. If she is slightly rejected by a friend, my abandonment fears need not overwhelm the situation. Her mild rejection is not my profound rejection in my alcoholic household. Difficult as it is, I will attempt to maintain some perspective. If I try to meddle and control things, I will perhaps weaken my child because I will not allow her to handle it in a way that feels right to her. If she feels rejected, I can simply comfort her and show her by my behavior that I will not reject her. Only if the situation is really out of control will I interfere and only after a personal inventory of my own issues.

I allow my child to live her life.

Everything happens to everybody sooner or later if there is time enough.

George Bernard Shaw

Today I recognize that the words I say to my children are not necessarily all that they hear. They are like a litmus paper for my unfinished business. What I refuse to see within myself shows up in them or in my relationship with them. It is not what I say to my children but who I am that carries the strongest message. Words can be used to communicate or as a smoke screen. They would be better off living with the truth than being told only what we wish were the truth. When there is too much disparity between what children feel is true and what they are told is true, they wonder why they can't get their inner reality and their outer reality to synchronize.

**I will protect my children by
giving them the truth.**

My tongue swore but my mind was still unpledged.

Euripides

Children think in magical ways. It is hard for them to believe that their parents ever existed before them. Children wonder if babies are stacked up in their mother's stomach and born when the parents want another brother or sister for them. They think that the sun is an orange ball and the moon is a white circle. When parents fall apart, children feel that they have the power to put them back together again. When parents are angry, children feel it is because they are bad. Children who have parents who constantly act out internalize a deep sense of failure.

I understand that my child might think in "magical" ways.

Humpty Dumpty sat on a wall
Humpty Dumpty had a great fall
All the king's horses
And all the king's men
Couldn't put Humpty together again.

Mother Goose

*T*oday I am grateful for my deep innocence. Much of my life I have felt old inside, as if I knew things before my time. Lately I have felt that all this knowledge has led, oddly enough, to a restoration of my innocence. I feel a real acceptance for life as it is. I understand that growth cannot be rushed; that the seasons will not come sooner if I drum my fingers on the table and that the sun will not set at my behest but rather at the close of day. I accept that in this world understanding and compassion will be the only true sword to do battle with. There is a peace in accepting life as it comes and not as I feel it ought to be. My children are not here to prove anything to me but to unfold and grow.

Life is all right the way it is.

Experience, which destroys innocence, also leads one back to it.

James Baldwin

Today I recognize my child's need to defy me. Part of her process of growing up and breaking away is to position herself in opposition to me. She is moving from the deeply dependent place of a child who defined herself alongside me to a person looking for somewhere else to be. Her first step is to state firmly that she is *not* me. The vehemence of her need comes from her profound dependence on me. It is not a rejection of me, but a search for her own place in the world. She is crawling out of my skin and into her own. As an ACoA I see this as a personal rejection and I return to my own deep feelings of abandonment. I had thought that finally I had someone who would not leave me but today I know that she is just reaching out for her own spirit. She may return, but first I must let her search.

God bless you on your quest.

Deep experience is never peaceful.

Henry James

Today I do not hold it against my children when they don't accept what I say just because I say it. It is natural for them to want to see and feel if fire really burns. Part of my job as parent is to guide them and give them the benefit of my experience and wisdom. I can do that by placing them in situations that are positive for them and steering them in directions that will be growth-producing. Having done this, I will stand by and let them find their way. I am there for support, nurturing or a gentle push; I am not there to measure how well they follow my directions. They need to take this time to build their own set of directions — ones that are right for their lifetime. They have a right to their own dreams.

I recognize that the true teacher is direct experience.

A proverb is no proverb till life has illustrated it.

John Keats

*T*oday I will feel the feelings of hurt, anger, shame, abandonment and resentment that are my inheritance from growing up in a dysfunctional family. My family became dysfunctional because they refused to feel these feelings. No matter what went on, the family rule was not to talk about it. *No talk.* If we don't talk, it will go away; it won't be there. If I did disclose my true feelings, everything was blamed on me, and I became a scapegoat for the family pain. So I learned to maintain a painful and costly silence. When I awaken painful feelings in recovery, a part of me is still tempted to silence them, to deny and minimize them because that is what worked for me in my past. Today I know it doesn't really work for me at all.

Today I will feel my feelings.

You can't heal what you can't feel.

Sharon Wegscheider-Cruse

Today I make no apologies. I am tired of feeling guilty all the time. In fact guilt is such a subtle and constant part of my mentality that I hardly identify it anymore. It just feels like a growing sense that I should be doing something I'm not doing or that there is something that I am not doing quite right. I have the right not to make things better. If someone doesn't seem to like me all that much, I don't need to spend my time being nice and trying to get them to see the good in me. It is not a sign of my coldness as a person not to care about what other people think of me; it is a freedom that I have a right to. It feels so good and unco-dependent to walk through life knowing that I can say no, that I am not in some invisible way at other people's beck and call.

"No, thank you" is a wonderful sentence.

Misery acquaints a man with strange bedfellows.

William Shakespeare

*T*oday I see denial for what it is — a misguided attempt to wipe the slate clean and maintain the status quo or the image of what we think we should be. We all have things we would rather not admit and would like to erase. Unfortunately those things we minimize and deny actually happened to some degree or another and when we erase them, we erase a part of ourselves. We need access to all of ourselves to live fully. The feelings that we refuse to feel are still in the atmosphere and our children end up feeling them for us unwittingly because they internalize the shame, anger or resentment as their own.

I lift the veil of denial.

Then we shall rise
And view ourselves with clearer eyes
In that calm region where no right
Can hide us from each other's sight.

Henry King

Today I will not be afraid to make mistakes and I will allow my child to make lots of them. How can he grow, learn and explore without "goofing up" now and then? Today when he makes a mistake, I will say, "It's good to make mistakes. It means you are not afraid to try." If I do not feel free to make mistakes, I become unable to take risks, and if I am unable to take risks, I am unable to make changes. If I cannot change, I "settle." I become set in my ways and wonder why nothing new ever happens to me. If my children see me trying new things and making mistakes, then they will feel free to do the same. I will give them a great gift — the freedom to fail.

**I let myself and my children
experience the freedom
to mess up.**

When I make a mistake — it's a beaut!

Fiorello LaGuardia

I grew up with co-dependency in my home. I keep waiting for it to change. Today I know that that is part of the family disease. I am the only one I have any control over — I can change. Trying to change my family so that I will feel I have a right to a decent life is my disease. Co-dependency as a family illness has a presence of its own. It is a system of dysfunctional agreements, expectations, rules and labels. It is a group experience of mutual abandonment, shame, pain, anger and resentment. It is a monster that lives in the closet, making its presence felt but not understood. Today I will deal with my own part of the family disease so that I do not pass it on to my children.

I deal with my part of the family disease.

Living well is the best revenge.

George Herbert

Today I value a steady and constant kind of love. I am deeply fortunate to have people in my life who have loved me through good and bad times. To love and leave and love and leave and love and leave is a sad repetition of a cycle of pain. There is a kind of strength and calm in being able to give love and accept love. My children seem to have this capacity naturally. It is such a challenge to simply live with love on a day-to-day basis. That kind of all-around love is a quiet thing.

I can live with love in my life.

Whoever loves, if he do not propose
The right true end of love, he's one that goes
To sea for nothing but to make him sick.

John Donne

I will live with balance in my world today. I will neither retreat from myself nor move into isolation. I will not cling to a friend nor will I ignore one. My children will be encouraged to live with balance in our home. Their friends will be truly welcome and encouraged; at the same time I will leave space for them to be with themselves. I will not shut them out in silence but will respect their privacy when they choose it. I will stand behind their school experience and be aware and involved but I will not live in the middle of it. Each year I will back up a little farther and let them experience working things out for themselves. I will listen.

I look for balance in our lives.

I had three chairs in my house; one for solitude, two for friendship, three for society.

Henry David Thoreau

Today I live this day as if I knew that my time here was limited. All of our lives will end in this form but we live as if we will be here forever. What am I saving it up for? Why not, as my child does, spend all my energy today? Reality is always heightened but I get hypnotized by the ordinariness of my routines. I accept that what I see when I open my eyes is all there is and I look to anchor myself somewhere in my schedule or my possessions or position rather than within my own invisible depths. When I am present within myself, I experience life differently. From this place I am able to be with my child because children live close to themselves. My way into their world is to live close to myself.

I center myself and experience.

The great art of life is sensation, to feel that we exist, even in pain.

Lord Byron

Today I know that what I see with my heart is what is true. My eyes deceive me. I recall the story of "The Emperor's New Clothes." Only the child believed what he saw — that the emperor had no clothes on. I will not ask my child not to know what he knows. I will not, for the sake of social convention or my own desires, blot out his truth and force mine down his throat. I will not make him separate too soon, nor will I ask him to need me more than he does and humiliate and weaken him in his quest for autonomy. I will let him tell me who he is. I will resist the urge to zip him into the personality that I like every morning. First I will observe him, then we'll talk about it.

I will not rob my child's truth from him.

Seeing is believing, but feeling is the truth.

Thomas Fuller

Today I will not rush through what I do. When I feel myself trying to push, I will center myself and slow down. Nothing is generally gained when I rush; a lot is lost. My child should not be rushed. His sense of time is different from mine and if I hurry him, it will feel to him as if I am tuned out to his world and don't understand him. He may even think that I am a little stupid and can't figure things out properly. I also cannot rush my child's development. If I try to push him, he will not be able to explore fully and move through each stage and will have to make it up later. Each stage fully experienced becomes another firm set of blocks in the foundation of who he will be, who he is becoming.

I will give time a chance.

People in a hurry cannot think, cannot grow, nor can they decay. They are preserved in a state of perpetual puerility.

Eric Hoffer

Today I will pay attention to the words I use with my children. We focus on physical forms of abuse and speak out against them but we forget the potential abuse of both silence and ill-considered words. I have such power in my child's life. She believes what I say to be true at some deep level. Silence can be equally painful when I leave her in that place of emptiness and refuse to communicate with her, leaving her with her frightened imagination. Words and silence are powerful communicators. Today I understand how important it is to communicate honestly with my children in a straightforward manner.

Silence and words are powerful communicators.

Many men are like unto sausages; whatever you stuff them with, that they will bear in them.

Alexei Tolstoi

Today I will try to understand what my child is saying to me. There is such a thing as misunderstanding; in fact it happens all the time. There was little allowance for misunderstanding where I grew up. We all took our positions, stayed there and defended them. Listening to the other person's point of view and trusting that there was any truth to it wasn't how we operated. Nor did we tell each other when we felt hurt. We really didn't communicate our own thoughts and feelings with one another; consequently I always felt that to get along I had to agree with everyone. A first step toward building trust is to really listen to what my children are saying.

You have something that I wish to hear.

As scarce as truth is, the supply has always been in excess of the demand.

Josh Billings

Today I know that healing past wounds is possible. When through whatever means my own internal healer is tapped, mysterious forces move within and around me and allow healing to take place. When a doctor opens a wound to let it drain, he has to depend on the body's own resources to complete the healing. Likewise with the emotions, when an emotional-psychic wound is opened and spills out in the form of words, tears or action, the natural healer within allows the new comfort, inner quiet and healing to take place. When I heal old childhood wounds like this, I bring a different parent to my children. I bring a parent who can parent a child.

I heal my childhood wounds.

Once drinking deep of that divinest anguish, how could I seek the empty world again?

Emily Bronte

Today I entertain all possibilities. There is a layer of possibility vibrating in the atmosphere and I connect with that when I quiet my mind and open my senses. Nothing is ever just one way and no situation is too difficult to be improved. I am here to learn from life, to integrate the lessons and grow, then to let go and move on. I actually think that as I forgive and forget, my brain changes shape so that I am not so much the sum total of my experiences and memories, but the sum total of my integrated learning. This makes life an exciting process full of potential for change, growth and movement.

I am open to that which I cannot see.

Become a possibilitarian. No matter how dark things seem to be or actually are, raise your sights and see the possibilities — always see them, for they're always there.

Norman Vincent Peale

Today I will just be myself with my children. I will not set an example; I will not be my image of what I should be. If I model anything today, it will be that I have the courage to be myself. I will say the wrong thing with my child, then backtrack and apologize. When I go slightly over the edge, I will come back to them, excuse myself, tell them I was out of line and explain to them that I had a tiring day, that sometimes I have trouble living with the power of my own feelings and that I will try to do better next time. When in being who I am I make a mistake, I will promptly admit it and make amends. I will not try to be something that I am not really capable of being and I will not ask that of them.

I model being who I am.

Kiss the hand of him who can renounce what he has publicly taught.

Johann Kaspar Lavater

Today I cast my gaze beyond the horizon and trust that something is there for me, that life wishes to hold and love me. Though I have had painful experiences, today I see them as lessons. I have learned and grown from everything I have gone through; these learnings have increased my depth and my value to myself and my children. When my son goes fishing, he casts his line as far out as he can. He is happy for all the bites he gets. He casts out for the pleasure of it and enjoys the anticipation of what might come. Often he throws the fish back. What does that tell me about my life? What I think I want, I often throw back too. I love the pleasure of this process of setting goals and growing and meeting them and throwing back the results.

I enjoy the process.

I look to the hills from whence doth my help come, my help cometh from the Lord who hath made all things, he will not suffer my foot to be moved.

The Bible

*T*oday I will be where I really am. I will tell the truth told to me. So often I know what I would like to say but the words just wander around my mind and never find their way out of my mouth. Maybe if I let people know who I am inside and what I really think more often, I would be less confusing to myself and to them and communication would be clearer. There is no reason why I cannot share my thought patterns with another person. I will not be afraid to let my children see the real me. Why should they have to wonder what is going through my mind when I can so easily tell them? I can help them to learn about who they are by sharing my thoughts with them openly.

I include my children in on my thinking.

The art of life is to show your hand. There is no diplomacy like candor. Nothing is so boring as having to keep up a deception.

E.V. Lucas

Today I remember that thoughts are actions. My thoughts are measurable through the use of sensitive instruments. The mind is also a sensitive instrument and picks up thoughts from other people all of the time. When we feel something is "in the atmosphere," it really is — tension, peace, fear, anger and love. These things need not be spoken to be felt. It is so important that I think well of my child, that I have faith and trust that things will work out for him. Because my thoughts are unspoken expectations, they have power in their silence. I have nothing to lose and everything to gain by thinking in a positive way about my children.

**I think positive thoughts
about my child.**

Give peace a chance.

John Lennon

Today I will carefully disregard my children's "proper size". I will allow them a little bit of healthy narcissism. I will not think them vain and stuck on themselves when they look at themselves in the mirror for seemingly endless hours or talk constantly about clothes, their interests or themselves. How can my children find life exciting if they don't find themselves exciting? What might look like vanity to me may be just a part of their process of getting to know themselves. If I trim them down too soon, they might take it to mean that I do not like them when they like themselves and fully explore their inner limits. Today I will let my children fall in love with themselves.

I endorse my child's self love.

show me a person not full of herself and i'll show you a hungry person.

nikki giovanni

Today I am going to correct my side of a difficult interaction and let go of the rest. If I take responsibility for what I bring to the arena of relating, it is enough. I really cannot change anyone else. Getting tied up in that kind of thinking is not helpful and is a pattern that I need to break. I will put this new one in its place — to look instead at my own behavior and in doing so with self-honesty free myself from it. It is the entanglement within myself that clouds my vision and leads to self-loathing. If I straighten out my own thinking, that in itself will be an action. If I bring a clear head to the situation, I have done my part and the rest will take its course, but my participation in it will have changed.

I clear up my own side of things.

I invent nothing. I rediscover.

Auguste Rodin

Today I will not obsess about the future but will trust that if I live well today, the future will naturally take care of itself. Plans and goals provide me with a sense of continuity, direction and security, but having laid them, I need to learn to let them go and free myself so that I can be present for today. I used to seek safety in plans but I do not require that to get through today. I have learned that the spiritual riches in life lie at my feet in this moment. My children are here today. I will not trade the experience of really being with them for a mental construct of ideas and rationales. I could float around in my mental processes forever but my children teach me that real life is happening right here, on the ground.

I release my obsessions.

I will not leave you comfortless.

The Bible

Today I examine the question of intimacy as it applies to me and to my relationship with my children. There is no one way to be intimate; there is no one road toward intimacy. It begins with my relationship to myself. How well do I know myself? How thoroughly can I tolerate my own feelings? Do I know and accept my strengths and weaknesses or am I conducting a relationship with myself based on who I wish I were? If I am comfortable with myself and willing to live with myself the way I am, I can allow that in someone else. To the extent to which I live with truth within myself, I bring truth and honesty to those I care about.

I have the strength to tolerate myself.

The face in the mirror of the mind, and eyes without speaking confess the secrets of the heart.

St. Jerome

Today I recognize the effect that living in a technological global village has on me and my children. The message to conform is very powerful. This is not necessarily good or bad but is something I need to be aware of if I want to be in a position to make individual choices for myself and my children. I can live on two levels — I can adapt socially and also let society adapt to me. I can lead in quietly constructive ways. I cannot knuckle under to negativity and pessimism. I can keep my eyes focused on the light and bring it in. My children have a spontaneous enthusiasm and positivity that they bring to this life with them. I can nurture that and let them nurture it in me.

There is plenty of room to be myself.

to be nobody but yourself — in a world which is doing its best, night and day, to make you everybody else — means to fight the hardest battle which any human being can fight, and never stop fighting.

e e cummings

Today I recognize my own individuality. I see where I leave off and the world begins. If I am truly to live a life tailored to me, it will be a suit that fits me perfectly. It will bend where I bend, go in and out where I go in and out. It will not be a good fit for anyone else. In this way I choose to tailor my life to the shape of my own personality. My likes and dislikes, needs and desires are unique to me. My children are equally their own people. Their friends, activities, schools and professions will be choices made from their perspective. I will try to make choices that will bring out the best in them and give them what they need until they are old enough to guide their own lives.

I am fully my own person.

I think Dostoevski was right, that every human being must have a point at which he stands against culture, where he says, this is me and the damned world can go to hell.

Rollo May

Today I am free of other people's stuff. For so long I lived in a situation that was unpredictable and unsettling. I tried to second-guess the moods of others in an attempt to protect myself from their changeability. In doing this over time I became more connected to other people's minds than my own. I became sensitive to the ups and downs of everyone but lost a sense of myself. I lost myself somewhere in the midst of other people. I don't do that today and I don't create a home that trains my children to do it either. When I do, I promptly admit that I am wrong and make amends. With the help of a Higher Power I am able to change.

**I manage my own life and
let other people manage theirs.**

Truth does not blush.

Tertullian

Today I will attempt to keep the focus on myself. In the past when that was suggested to me, I felt a mixture of sadness and anger; partly for a self I sensed I had lost and partly for a self I had no idea where to find. Today I understand it as a blueprint for sane living — anything we take care of, we come to know and understand, whether it be a child, a business or a garden. Wouldn't the same follow for a self? Perhaps if I take care of myself, I will come to know better who I am. If I listen and respond to the inner me, I will find out who is there. When I do this, I can come to see my children not as an extension of myself but as separate selves.

Today I keep the focus on myself.

A show of envy is an insult to oneself.

Yevgeny Yevtushenko

*T*oday I recognize that recovery requires a leap of faith. First comes belief and conception on my part. Once I can imagine how I would like my life to be, I can begin to take the necessary steps to guide it toward that goal. The same is true for my children. I need to believe in their happiness. They are held by their own Higher Power and they have a positive destiny. Their lives have meaning not only to me but to themselves and the world they inhabit. I believe in their essential goodness and that is what will manifest in their lives. My children will be taken care of and will have what they need.

I believe in the goodness of life.

Seek not to understand that you may believe, but believe that you may understand.

St. Augustine

Today I believe in life. I cast my heart into the wind and let it become one with its ultimate good. I replace the fear inside myself with love of life. No matter who or what has hurt and disillusioned me today, that will not stop me being how I want to be within myself. I will not ask life to prove itself to me today in order for me to feel comfortable. This is the attitude I will arm my children with — gratitude, optimism and courage. I will show them what these concepts mean through my own attitude and behavior. Life is beautiful when I decide it is beautiful. If I give my children everything material but no love of life, they will be always searching, always vaguely dissatisfied.

I love life today.

In spite of everything, I still believe that people are really good at heart.

Anne Frank

221

Today I will remember that amid all that
I do and wish for my child, it is my pre-
vailing attitude that will seep in at the deepest level. It doesn't matter if I hand the world
to my child on a silver platter if my heart is
not a part of the offering. The gift that my
child truly understands is the gift of myself,
my presence, my love and understanding. I
will not let either of us be seduced by anything else. If I am not able to share myself
with my child, then her hands will come up
empty and nothing that I hand to her short
of me will really fill them. Even if I am not
perfect, I am all that I have and all that she
has, so I will not hold back.

I will give what I have to give.

More kindness will do nothing less
Than save every sleeping one
And nightwalking one of us.

James Dickey

Today I will let the sadness of my past drain from my heart and soul. I will not carry it in silence, a secret even from myself in an effort to look good or superior or all together. To be truly together I need to live comfortably with all of my parts, not just the polished few that I would take with me to a cocktail party. My grief is real. If I do not mourn my past hurts, I will recreate them over and over again in a blind attempt to feel them at last. There is really no repression in this sense — only the eyes of the conscious mind and the eyes of the unconscious mind. We may shut our conscious eyes but our unconscious eyes remain open and searching for our own truths — a place to be, to settle and to rest.

I will grieve when I need to.

All through the dark the wind looks for the grief it belongs to.

William Stanley Merwin

Today I recognize the joy that comes into my life, around and through me. You are a deep and powerful source of life and love and joy. In some ways you know more about life than I do because you allow yourself to experience it more fully. I am forever mistaking life for ideas about life. I swim around in a mental factory of rationales and thoughts, I organize and reorganize perception and I call it living. I am two utensils removed from my food. Direct experience is the only real thing. It changes every chemical in my body to feel at a deeper level. This is what my child does naturally. How truly exciting!

I open myself to direct experience.

That's joy, it's always a recognition, the known appearing fully itself, and more itself than one knew.

Denise Levertov

*T*oday I give myself the time I need to grow and I give my children the time they need to grow. I seem to want to look at my children and see what they will be rather than what they are now. I want to be assured that the finished product will be okay. Whatever made me think that it was ever finished? I am still building myself, still hoping, dreaming, wondering what the future holds. I will not rush my children anymore. They have plenty of time to become a thousand different things. Today I'll enjoy them for being just where they are, knowing that they are busy building the person they are becoming.

I accept my child where he is today.

The game ain't over 'till it's over.

Yogi Berra

Today if I hurt my children in any deep way at any time, I resolve that I will ask them for their forgiveness. I ask not only because I want to be forgiven but to remove the thorn of hatred for me from their hearts. To have hatred and resentment for the parent damages the child's heart. It is for me to show them the way of love and forgiveness. This is a gift to my children and my grandchildren. I have no intention of letting my children abuse me, but I will do everything I can to keep the door in their soul of love for their parent open. Today I have the humility to accept this gift and to respect it as such.

I humbly ask my children's forgiveness when I hurt them.

Man must evolve for all human conflict a method which rejects revenge, aggression and retaliation. The foundation of such a method is love.

Martin Luther King, Jr.

*T*oday I will allow my children to experience sexual feelings. Freud made a great contribution in getting the world to accept that children are sexual beings. They need not feel embarrassed about their bodies and the sensations they experience. It is important in life to feel good about your sexuality and I will not send silent messages to my children that make them go into hiding. I will not in any way be provocative with my children or meet my sexual needs through them in whatever form. Nor will I push them away as they develop out of fear of the feelings of attraction aroused in me. I am comfortable with myself as a sensual, sexual being and I model that for my children.

I allow my children to be sexual, sensual beings.

Freud found sex an outcast in the outhouse, and left it in the living room an honored guest.

W. Beran Wolfe

Today I will be conservative. Rather than think in terms of using things up, I will think in terms of appreciating what I have. I will truly understand my custodial role on this earth. We have inherited a world badly abused. Those who took advantage of nature's gifts didn't understand what they were doing or didn't care, but today it is imperative that I do understand. First, I will teach my children to love this world, its natural and cultural variety and beauty. No one likes to see what they love get hurt or disappear. In a way it is more unifying to preserve simply for its own sake and that of future generations than to get what we can.

I believe that this earth has a future.

My life belongs to the world. I will do what I can.

James Dickey

Today I will be a friend to my child. When she talks to me, I will listen and show an interest. When my child needs to talk to someone, I want her to feel that she can talk to me; that if she opens her heart to me, I will not abuse it. What a beautiful thing to have a friendship with this person who is born from me, to let her grow and be a parent to her but to also develop a friendship alongside so that we will be able to have a long-lasting relationship! After adolescence when my child has declared her independence, she does not want a parent fussing around her. She wants one who can stand back and be present for her as a parent when she needs one. Today I am going to learn how to be that friend and consciously develop a friendship with my child.

I befriend my child.

A faithful friend is the medicine of life.

The Bible

Today I do not presume to teach anyone else what I cannot first teach myself. "Do as I say, not as I do" is worthless. What I do is what counts. Who I am is what will teach my children, not what I say. One characteristic that I display clearly in my behavior over and over again will teach them more than thousands of well-chosen words. I am telling them by my behavior that I don't believe in what I say. They will learn this underlying lesson and little else, and I will cut my effectiveness with them in half. My children are not that demanding. If they see that I am willing to be human and trying to do my best, they will probably forgive me the rest, be relieved that they can be human too and forgive themselves their shortcomings.

I let my children see who I am.

Physician, heal thyself.

The Bible

*T*oday I give myself the space I require to have my feelings. My feeling of being easily abandoned makes me reactive when that button is pushed in me. I get frightened and want to run away while at the same time I want to rush toward whoever I feel is abandoning me and fall at their feet. The hysterical child within me rules me at those times and my adult self disappears. First I need to acknowledge the depth of my fear — I can measure it by the extent of my reactiveness. Next I need to give myself time to feel these feelings when they are activated and neither react by running away nor by trying to make things all better. My huge reaction, however, does me no good and makes me always appear the one "out of control."

I stand straight up and feel my feelings.

I think that people want peace so much that one of these days government had better get out of their way and let them have it.

Dwight D. Eisenhower

*T*oday I will pay attention to what I say to my children. My child believes in me and in what I say. I remember how much what my parents said meant to me. Carl Rogers says that one of the most important factors in therapy is the "positive regard of the therapist" for the client. This is what my child needs from me — my positive regard. She needs to feel that underneath it all I think well of her, that I feel that she can do things, take care of herself and reach her goals. I will not withhold my good opinion from my child, nor will I give it but in measured doses so that I can use it to manipulate her. My positive regard is hers; she does not have to deserve or earn it.

I think and speak well of my child.

Many have fallen by the edge of the sword, but not so many as have fallen by the tongue.

The Bible

Today I will "live" and not "do". Just for today I will reclaim my life. I will let obligations slide, get little done of great import. I will relax and give my mind and my body a break. I have a tendency to become co-dependently involved with activity. I don't want to miss anything. I feel things will not get done if I don't do them. In recovery I recognize that these feelings are born of the constant insecurity in my past — of growing up in a situation that felt volatile and unstable. I always felt I wasn't doing enough to get things back to normal, to make it right. I carry this compulsion into my life today but I am going to change it beginning right now. I will be a better person and a better parent if I can allow myself the freedom not to act, not to be constantly busy and doing. I am free to choose how I spend my time.

My day belongs to me.

Be thine own palace or the world's thy jail.

John Donne

Today I will explore my limits and allow my children to explore theirs. There is "such a lot of living to do," so why not do it? What am I waiting for? I don't mean that I have to run through the streets or go on a shopping spree. I want to live without trimming off the edges, to feel without running my feelings through a series of questionnaires, to do something novel and show up for life as myself. My children have a wonderful ability to give fully and freely. I think I did too when I was young. When did I get so controlled and controlling? When did I forget that these precious children will not be with me forever — that each day we have together is a gift?

I will live and grow today — right now.

If the unexamined life is not worth living, then the unlived life is not worth examining.

Zerka Moreno

Today I will not solve the problems of the world in my head over and over again. I am aware of all the world's problems on a daily basis — they enter my home and heart through television, newspaper, radio and so on. Some days it's just too much. I worry about the world that my children are inheriting. Just for today I will not take all this on my shoulders and will adopt an attitude of optimism. Whatever will happen in the future, the world can only be helped by my attitude of quiet optimism. My children deserve to take a positive attitude toward their lives and world — they need that. They also need to feel that I not only believe in them but in their world as well.

I am optimistic about this world.

I refuse to accept the cynical notion that nation after nation must spiral down a militaristic stairway into the hell of nuclear destruction. I believe that unarmed truth and unconditional love will have the final word in reality.

Martin Luther King, Jr.

Today I accept that life is not permanent. I live as if life were forever, as if I had endless time to waste. When I live with the awareness that life as I know it is not permanent, I appreciate it much more. Suddenly the humdrum world that I take for granted seems imbued with a kind of pulsating life and spiritual energy that I am not in touch with at other times. My children are not mine forever either — so quickly they will grow up and go away. These years that we have together are fleeting; what I don't do with them now will probably not get done. If I want a close relationship with them in the future, I need to work on it today. That is how it will be there later — because it was here today.

I live knowing that life is temporary.

When wings are grown, birds and children fly away.

                                        Chinese Proverb

Today I am not going to base everything I do in my life on everyone's needs but mine. I will not hold my life in the balance of the lives around me anymore. My needs are important too. When I do not address any of my own needs, I only end up resenting those I live with. My children will not benefit from watching me model doormat behavior. How will they figure out how to have a life and a family if even I can't do it? Often I feel as if I have to choose between the two, but today I am going to try something different. I am going to imagine that there is room for us all to have identities and lives of our own. If I lose my identity and fuse it with that of my spouse and children, I will feel like a functionary and not a person. Today I am here. I matter.

There is room for all of us to matter.

Rancor is an outpouring of a feeling of inferiority.

Jose Ortega y Gasset

Today if I sense that people in my life are underfunctioning, I will not overfunction to fill in the gap. If other people disappear emotionally, it is not up to me to search for them in the darkness of their own soul or the vacuum of their own personality. Their search is their search and when I spend my time looking for someone else, I lose myself in the process. I have my own search. Sometimes it is a good thing to lose one's self in a spiritual quest but that is different from the loss that happens when I cannot tolerate not knowing exactly where those around me are. It is my job to know where I am; chasing after other people, places and things will only postpone my being with myself. Being engaged in everyone else's business is a good smoke screen in which I can hide from myself.

I feel my own feelings, not everybody else's.

Let there be spaces in your togetherness.

Kahlil Gibran

Today I know that I do not need to wait for my parents to become healthy people to heal my deep grief at having lost them. Those are the unshed tears of my inner child, the sadness at having to watch the people I loved so much disappear into themselves, the terror and fright I felt at seeing that I had to rely on myself and not knowing how. I have carried those feelings into my adulthood in the form of a pool of loneliness, desperation and paranoia. Today I know that I do not need my parents' permission to feel these feelings and let them go. If I am willing to return to this place of grief and terror, then I can walk out again, with a strength that I didn't have before. I can let good things in to that now emptied space.

I can heal on my own.

Above all, do not lose your desire to walk.

Soren Kierkegaard

Today I understand my need for control.
When my parents felt far away from me
as a child, I needed to find any way I could
to pull them into my reach. Drama worked
the best and for that moment I felt less
alone. I made contact, I got their interest.
Unfortunately, I am still doing that as an
adult, ignoring myself until my inner child
creates a drama or throws a tantrum before
I finally take care of myself and pay attention to what I am feeling. I need to listen to
myself as I would like to have been listened
to as a child, to care about what I am feeling
as I wish someone would have cared about
the way I felt when I was growing up. That
kind of constant uncertainty need not haunt
me in my life today. I don't have to live in
fear of abandonment if I learn not to abandon myself.

I am steady and reliable.

Trust your hopes, not your fears.

David Mahoney

Today I will sing the song that is in my soul. I will reach beyond myself, I will extend my arms outwards, look toward the hills, think and hope, pray and dream. I will not sit on my heart today or be run by my needs, my past and my compulsions. Why should I forever be in blindness? What is the worst thing that could happen if I dare to feel that there might be more, if I reach into the dark and shadowy nothingness within myself, grab onto it and pull it into the light? Why should I live in silence to my own self, parading what I know well, pretending that it is enough and all there is? Today I will have a conversation with the teacher who lives within me. I will open my eyes and heart to my child. I will not hide away.

**I recognize my own soul
and the souls of my children.**

Call the world if you please "The vale of soul-making."

John Keats

*T*oday I understand that I was born deeply
dependent. It is no wonder that it was so
terrifying when I stopped being able to depend on my parents. Eventually I became
frightened and ashamed of my needs. I have
taken this into adulthood with me as a feeling that no one can really understand me or
my pain. But as I look back it seems so ob-
vious and uncomplicated. It is the wall that I
have built around those feelings that is so
complicated and hard to dismantle. It is made
of self-delusion, unspoken grief, resentment
and fear. It is when I can take down my own
wall, return to the innocent state that I was
once in and feel what that child felt that I
can find myself and my Higher Power.
There is a purity in pain that is fully felt.
Purity and innocence belong to my child and
my Higher Power.

I can face the full extent of my pain.

*Unless you become like a child you cannot enter the
kingdom of heaven.*

The Bible

Today I can separate the parent I had as a child from the parent I have today. People change. If my parent has something to give me today, why shouldn't I accept it? Perhaps it feels too risky or I am too angry to let them know I still care. The child within me may be the one who is in the most pain and needs to grieve the loss of the parents who weren't there. As the recovering person I am today, I can stand by my inner child while she walks through the terrible pain and terror that she felt. I can acknowledge the full extent of my loss as a young person, mourn it and move on. My pain as a child need not to be my pain as an adult anymore; I can see it for what it is.

**I mourn my past and release
myself from its grip.**

Think of a big color — who cares if people call you Rothko. Release your childhood. Release it.

Larry Rivers and Frank O'Hara

Today I accept my life as a long road with ups and downs. I have had all sorts of experiences, some painful, some joyous; a myriad of subtle changes woven together to make my life. My child's life is the same. She already has seen much of living and each thread is woven to the others to create what is and will be her life. We are on a continuum together. Beginning and ending seem almost an illusion when I let this awareness of the vicissitudes of time wash over me. Events seem like part of an overall picture or pattern. It's nice to feel a part of something continuing.

I accept life as a pattern.

What is more enthralling to the human mind than this splendid, boundless, colored mutability! Life in the making?

David Grayson

Today I wonder why I over-parent. I am so worried that my children might have an unmet need that I over-respond to their signals. As a child, while my family illness progressed, many of my needs went unmet. I tried to hide it from myself at the time by pretending that it didn't matter. Today I still have trouble identifying a genuine need and responding to it. I may just be bored and need a minor change of activity, but instead I adopt the feeling that my life is somehow a mess. It is difficult for me to separate one need from another and see it for what it is — a simple need. It is just as hard for me to do this with my children. All of their needs seem pressing to me and I swing into action to meet them before I even decide if they ought to be met, postponed or put aside.

I will develop a need hierarchy in myself and with my children.

The most important thing that parents can teach their children is how to get along without them.

Frank Clark

Today I will lighten up. For so long it has been my habit to take things seriously, always looking for signs and symptoms of dysfunction. At some point in my recovery I need to understand the difference between denying trouble and creating it. Eventually I'll have to accept the possibility that my life actually can feel okay. No one's life is perfect but mine is NO LONGER in crisis. No one has any stake in keeping me down; it's time to release myself from my own self-imposed bondage. The way I perceive myself needs to change. My role of parent is not a sentence; it is a duty and one that I can define in a variety of ways. Being a family member is a serious role but one that I can thoroughly enjoy.

I will welcome a new kind of life.

Never believe that anyone who depends on happiness is happy. He who would be truly happy must think his own lot best, and so live with men, as considering that God sees him, and so speak to God, as if men heard him.

Seneca

Today I will honor what my parents gave me. So often when I am working through past pain, I remember all the deficits of my childhood — what I didn't get, what was missing. But today I treasure the beauty and the gifts that I grew up with. I am grateful for my life and I am proud of who I am. I have come a long way from where I began — so did my parents — and what they learned they taught me. It is so important for me to claim what was good and build on that within myself. I am in quiet possession of what felt genuinely good. This is what I can take to my positive life today and pass on with love and pride to my own children.

I am grateful for the good times.

Though I have looked everywhere, I can find nothing lowly in the universe.

A.R. Ammons

Today I recall my childhood point of view of my parents, that strange childlike combination of a mythical hero and a broken sparrow. How I sensed the pain and shame of my parents and how desperately I tried to fix their lives! I so wanted to weave or spin myself into a child who had magical healing powers so that I could heal them. I wanted to be special or great so that they would feel special and great and I could relax. I wanted to remove their pain and shame, to make our family clean and happy like other families seemed to be. At some level I really thought that I could do this, that it was my job and purpose in life.

**I accept my desperation
as a child vis-a-vis my parents.**

*For he seemed to me again like a king, like a king
    in exile,*
Uncrowned in the underworld,
Now due to be crowned again.
*Necessary, forever necessary, to burn out false
    shames.*

D. H. Lawrence

Today I accept that I am doing enough for my children. Because I felt under-nurtured as a child I have a tendency to overnurture my children. Gratifying all of my children's needs indiscriminately can be as damaging as not gratifying them. They will grow up with a distorted view of what they can expect from life, work, their own spouse and family. They will have the same vague feeling of never being satisfied that the person whose needs are undermet has. The natural way is in between — some needs are met, some postponed momentarily, some not met.

**First I will understand
my own needs and neediness.**

Love moderately; long love doth so.

William Shakespeare

Today I am grateful for the beauty and love I felt as a child. I would not know how to reach for recovery if I hadn't once known what I am reaching for. I was a child who was loved. Because I have my own children I understand how difficult it would be not to love your own child. I was a child in my parents' arms once. It is because I was loved that it hurt so desperately to be estranged from them. Today I understand that they were estranged from themselves through no fault of mine. They were unable to find themselves, each other and consequently me. I no longer need to continue that self-abandonment.

I remember the good times.

Dost thou wish to receive mercy? Show mercy to thy neighbor.

St. John Chrysostom

Today I will only seek to be a "good enough" parent. I will not try to raise my children perfectly, driving them and me into a mild state of frenzy. My children do not have to prove to the world that I am okay, nor do I have to prove anything to anyone about myself. I needn't push every lesson, skill and characteristic into my children that is out there; I also will not raise hot-house plants who are so overcared for that they can't survive in any environment but mine. My children need some space and so do I. We don't need to be ingrown to grow together; in fact if we grow too closely, we will inevitably be caught in each other's shade. As a "good enough" parent I will be satisfied with a "good enough" child.

I do not need to be perfect to be okay.

George Bernard Shaw warned Jascha Heifetz that the gods might envy his perfection and destroy him. Shaw advised the violinist to "play one wrong note every night before you go to bed."

Today I acknowledge that sometimes I feel overwhelmed by my role as parent. The responsibility of raising children and running a home can feel like too much to me. I fantasize about a life that is less humdrum where the buck stops somewhere other than on my lap. I create a good life for my children. It is basically stable, happy and their needs are well attended. I have worked so hard to achieve this that I can forget to attend to parts of my own life. Some of this is an occupational hazard of being a parent. Some of this is a result of my perceiving and acting on other people's needs and giving them precedence over mine.

Today I acknowledge feeling overwhelmed.

Here is how to live without resentment or embarrassment in a world in which you are different from everyone else: Be indifferent to the indifference.

Al Capp

*T*oday I honor you. I look at you and I am thrilled. You are the best of me and all of you. You are my gift to life, and life's gift to me, my noble purpose, the return to and from the greater self. I put bows in your hair. I walk hand in hand along the street with you, we bake cookies, we are smart, we are silly, you are the greatest love I have ever known. I can never express to you what you mean to me — only see it in my gaze, feel it in my touch, know it from the endless hours we pass in pleasure, understand it from the way in which I suffer when you suffer. My love for you is the best part of me. Thank you for coming.

You are my Princess.

Little Girl, my stringbean, my lovely Woman
I say Live, Live, because of the sun
The dream, the excitable gift.

Anne Sexton

Today I will not go through my life feeling as if I am missing something. There aren't a hundred places it would be better for me to be today — roads not travelled, things not done. Taking care of other people has the built-in occupational hazard of always feeling that I am not quite where I am supposed to be. Today I will not let my caretaker role rob me of my personality and personhood. If I want my children to eventually be free to be themselves, I need to let myself be free as well. I have confused healthy detachment with abandonment. What happened to me was not the result of parents living free and expressive lives; it was a result of their desperate flights *from* themselves, not *to* themselves, that left me in limbo.

Two whole people have a lot to give each other.

How simple and frugal a thing is happiness: a glass of wine, a roast chestnut, a wretched little brazier, the sound of the sea . . . All that is required to feel that here and now is a simple frugal heart.

Nikos Kazantzakis

Today I know that I do not choose to live as I grew up and that that is okay. It doesn't mean that any of us are bad or wrong. It only means that for a lot of different reasons we were not able to create and enjoy healthy family dynamics. It is not my family members as individuals that I have the most trouble with but the dynamics that get going when we are together. We do not play healthy roles for each other. I have to find my own way out of that; I can't expect a sick system to magically become healthy. But I can and will become healthy myself so that I can live a happier life and not recreate a sick system with my children. Getting healthy myself is the only way to improve my life or my family relationship, past or present.

I have a choice.

Stop going to the hardware store to buy grapefruit.

Al-Anon Saying

Today I understand the nature of denial in the disease of co-dependency. It is a disease that cannot say that it is a disease and has a constant need with other people to say that it is not a disease. In its denial of its existence it needs to convince itself that it is right and healthy. It appears in my life as an overattachment to my children and an inability to let them go and see them as people separate from me. I see it manifest in my own family when I seem to have no time or energy to meet my own needs because I am so busy meeting everyone else's and I'm not sure I would know what my needs are to begin with. It is seeing my children act out what I deny in myself.

I see symptoms for what they are.

The hero of my tale, whom I love with all the power of my soul, whom I have tried to portray in all his beauty, who has been, is and will be beautiful, is Truth.

Leo Tolstoi

You, precious babies, are a song in your mother's heart. It is part of life's exquisite mystery that a person can be born out of a person. I will never know or understand how this happens and I will never understand my love for you. I can only feel it and know that it is nature's and God's way of keeping us pure — to love something else more than we love ourselves. I love the way you run and jump and climb everything. Your need for space and activity, your love of movement, your wild and raucous energy amuse and challenge me and fill my heart. The love between us is for me like a gem of pure value — so deep, clear and strong. You give to me so generously and I appreciate it enormously. With all of my being, I love you and I know that you love me. Thank you.

I honor and protect your innocence.

The moment the little boy is concerned with which is a jay and which is a sparrow, he can no longer see the birds or hear them sing.

                                        Eric Berne

I understand today that it does not work for me to lose myself in the fabric of my family. I am more than the glue that holds us together. If I am not clear on this, then I run the risk of becoming the glue. I will be lost in the creases and crevices that I am filling and will lose my own solid core. No one will know where to find me because I will be a little bit in the empty spaces around everyone else and nowhere in particular. I may even cease to know where to find myself. Everything, every mood, every up and down of this family system is not my responsibility. If I hold everyone else up with various parts of myself, their extremities will atrophy from disuse and so will my core. I am not in this role to live everyone's life but mine. If I do that, I will be a role and not a person, and when my role changes, I will change. When my role is over, I will be over.

I am more than my role.

There's less here than meets the eye.

Tallulah Bankhead

Today I refuse to sell myself or my children any bill of goods that society and the media may come up with about what will make us happy. If it involves buying something or becoming something other than what I am, I will be suspicious. By now I understand that happiness is a byproduct of serenity and contentment which come when I learn to love and accept myself, not for what I could be but for who I am; and when I accept life, not for what it could potentially give me but for all that it does give by its very nature. My children are wonderful just the way they are. Why do we all need to be so different?

Today I will "be" rather than "do."

Treasure each other in the recognition that we do not know how long we shall have each other.

Joshua Liebman

Today I love because it is better to love than not to love. I don't wait to have life prove itself to me before I can love it. I don't wait for people to become who I want them to be before I can love them as they are. I don't love for pretense or habit or because someone told me to. When I love, I just love. In my life I choose love as given. My children need not work for my love; it is the one thing in their lives that I will give them no matter what. I will not ask them to twist themselves into a special shape to be worthy of my love.

I give and accept love for its own sake.

Beware of all the paradoxical in love. It is simplicity which saves. It is simplicity which brings happiness. Love should be love.

Charles Baudelaire

Today I respect my child's rhythm. She has her own approach to life, her own way of doing things. She needs to get to know herself, her ways and her pace. When she understands how she does things as a distinct entity, she will be in a better position to compromise with others because she'll recognize the necessity to do so. She can adjust herself without giving herself away and make compromises without compromising herself. If I control her whole life to avoid a little pain now, to make it all smooth in my eyes, I will set her up for pain later. She may not understand how to run her own life and look to others to run it for her — that could be risky. I would be training her to be co-dependent.

I allow my child to take charge wherever appropriate.

To behave with dignity is nothing less than to allow others freely to be themselves.

Sol Chaneless

Today I recognize that my children absorb not so much what I say but who I am. They are, in more ways than I care to see, containers for my unconscious. This is why it is so important for me to learn about what is really going on with me, to be willing to take responsibility for it and work with it. If I do not do this, I run the risk that I will project my unconscious fears and anxieties onto them rather than owning them myself. They can live with me far better knowing that I have weaknesses that I am aware of than they can live with those weaknesses assigned to them. That is called scapegoating and today I am not willing to do that to my child no matter how much work I have to do on myself to avoid it.

I own my unconscious.

Where is there dignity unless there is honesty?

Marcus Tullius Cicero

Today I will accept what feels good and nurturing rather than reject it. For so long I internalized a harsh nurturer. Today when something feels too good, I find it suspect. I reject it and look for something critical again. I reject what I truly say that I want in favor of what feels familiar to me. Without meaning to I pass on this harshness to my children too because what I cannot do for myself, I am also unable to do for them. I need not only to be kind to myself but to accept kindness into myself — to soften myself inside so that peace will have a chance. If I can take this in, I can give it to my children. I want this for all of us. I want to feel as sweet inside as their faces look to me. I want to give and receive — they are both blessed and part of the same divine dance.

I can accept kindness and love.

There is no failure except in no longer trying.

Elbert Hubbard

Today I will see criticism in a different light, both when I do it and when I receive it. After all, what is the point of criticizing others? There are ways of saying what needs to be said that don't wound — the need to wound is about something else. When I tell my children things, why should I be hurtful? If I put things in a way that makes them feel bad, they will have to put up a wall to defend themselves against being hurt. Because they are being defensive they won't hear what I am saying. They will then be left without the message and with a feeling that they have been criticized. I can find a better way to say things, and when I am criticized, I can see it differently.

Why should I be critical when I could be kind?

Criticism comes easier than craftsmanship.

Zeuxis

*T*oday I understand that love and forgiveness pave the road to happiness. I can express my anger and disillusionment, my pain, my hurt and loneliness and I need to. But if I do not then move it to a place of love and forgiveness, I will never really be free or have what I want in my life again. Forgiving is like releasing a freshwater spring within my own heart and soul. It is not that I owe this necessarily to others but I owe it to myself. The gift of forgiveness that we give to others is the gift that we give ourselves. The hand of mercy we extend is the hand that extends to us. The age-old spiritual truths are those that we struggle for and learn again and again. This life is really a life of the spirit infused by material and not the reverse.

I am glad to be here.

And in the end the love you take is equal to the love you make.

Paul McCartney

Today I will allow myself to trust in life. As a child the family I trusted became a living nightmare for me. I never knew if or when anything would happen. I learned, over time, not to trust, to hold myself back from hope and to discount myself and my dreams. I learned that the people closest to me could not necessarily be trusted and my environment became toxic to me. Today I am able to recognize what happened. Even being willing to live with this awareness teaches me something — that I can trust myself. I know where I am comfortable today — I can check in with myself. I can trust in my ability to know what is good for me and take action on my own behalf. I can be both caring and nurturing to myself and honest in guiding myself in ways of thinking and being that are beneficial to me.

I can learn to trust myself.

I am interested in this world, in this life, not some other world or future life.

Jawaharlal Nehru

Today I see that I can see my past as I choose to see it. Why should I dwell on pain any longer than I have to? The pain I had made me who I am; if living in a dysfunctional home doesn't kill something in you, it makes you a better person. It is that better person that I will take into life with me today; it is that better person that I will be. I am tired of focusing on the negative — it feels like time to let go, to let the past be history and to let my present be stronger and bigger than my past. It is time to change my habit of feeling the negative in my life more strongly than I feel the positive. Good feelings are my birthright too. Being deeply disappointed once in life does not mean that disappointment has to continue to be a constant theme for me. I can take the risk of feeling good about life today. I am strong enough to take what comes.

Life feels good today.

The tragedy of life is what dies inside a man while he lives.

Albert Schweitzer

Today I honor my child's journey inward. She is following a path that I am only a part of, searching out a person within that neither she nor I have as yet completely met. She has within her a deep inner world waiting to be discovered, waiting to be known. Many of the maturing processes she goes through I may have gone through already. I will reach down deep into myself for understanding so that I can join her. Not only will I observe from outside, but I will also support her from within — quietly — not usurping her experience but letting her know that others too have passed this way.

I acknowledge my child's search.

We are so engaged in doing things to achieve purpose of utter value that we forget that it is the inner value that is the rapture associated with being alive that it is all about.

Joseph Campbell

Today I feel that the secret to the whole thing is to love the life I have. There is something to this energy of love that is transforming. Why should I wish all the time to be somebody else or to live a different life? My children are fine just as they are. Why should I wish that they were different? There is life and beauty within me all of the time but I walk right by them. I avoid quiet but it is in silence that I am able to reach deeply enough inside of me to pull out that force of love with which I can nurture myself and those around me. I rush around as if there were somewhere more important to go than within my own heart. All that I need to be I already am. Today I will look inside.

I look within myself for myself.

We know the truth, not only by the reason, but by the heart.

Blaise Pascal

Today I understand that after years of struggling to make myself loveable and acceptable to family members who simply can't accept me, I can stop trying. For whatever reason it's not working. I can relax. It is not in my power to be okay for someone else; what I need is a clear conscience. If I know that I am willing to take responsibility for my stuff and that I am not feeling antagonistic toward someone else, what more can I do? I can offer my hand in peace but I have no control over whether or not it is taken. I cannot make anyone like me, but I can like myself. After all I am the one who has to live with me. And that's okay.

**I can be okay with
myself in spite of what others
feel toward me.**

Be yourself, that's all there is of you.

Ralph Waldo Emerson

Today I will hold my temper. Growing up in an alcoholic home, I learned to keep my feelings in — to sit on my natural and appropriate responses until they built up and finally blew. Blowing up was more acceptable in my home than honest communication. If I tried to talk about what I genuinely felt, I got hurt and I was cast out of the circle of family acceptance. The problem with talking about what I saw was that it was too real for a family in denial to hear or a parent in denial to tolerate. So I would wait until I couldn't hold it in any more, then throw a tantrum like everyone else did. Nothing was healed or resolved but there was a momentary relief. However, I went away filled with guilt and self-recrimination and a sense of having again failed. Today I can talk first and blow later.

**I really try to communicate
my feelings honestly in a way that
someone else can hear.**

All these woes shall serve for sweet discourses in our time to come.

William Shakespeare

Today I will remember that it is in giving that I clear my own pathway to receiving. If I am feeling blocked, I will consider this. Sometimes the best way to take care of myself is to get out of myself. Recovery is such a difficult balance. In the past, when I gave, it became distorted because in my dysfunctional family people were so incredibly needy. I did not feel acknowledged and appreciated for what I gave. In fact I felt that what I gave was never enough. I thought that if I gave what I wanted to receive, I would get it back — my needs would be met. Eventually what I learned was that my needs could be met but not necessarily by those people.

I have the strength and wisdom to give.

It is in giving that we receive.

The Bible

Today I recognize my need to heal the family that lives inside of me as a base to work from in creating my own. I will not necessarily be able to create healed, comfortable relationships with each family member but I can work through what is in the way for me and let go of the rest. Perhaps the relationships will heal in time or perhaps they won't but my side will be clean of the debris of held resentment, jealousy and hatred. I can only make myself different. I can't spend the rest of my life wishing for things not to be the way they are. I am able to live in the full reality of my life today. No one is perfect, no life is perfect but mine is good enough.

I am ready to accept my life as it is.

Never in this world can hatred be stilled by hatred; it will only be stilled by no-hatred — this is the Law Eternal.

Buddha

Today I feel that the secret to the whole thing is to love the life I have. There is something to this energy of love that is transforming. Why should I wish all the time to be somebody else or to love in a different life? My children are fine just as they are, why should I wish that they were different? There is life and beauty within me all of the time but I walk right by it. I avoid quiet but it is in silence that I am able to reach deeply enough inside of me to reach that force of love with which I can nurture myself and those around me. I rush around as if there were somewhere more important to go than within my own heart. All that I need to be I already am. Today I will look inside.

I look within myself for myself.

One word frees us of all the weight and pain of life. That word is love.

Sophocles

Today I feel like Emily in the last act of *Our Town*. Everything around me seems so temporary and at the same time very precious. I didn't realize how quickly time passed until my children began to grow up. If they are getting older, then I must be too. I really understand today how tragic it would be to wish any part of my life away. First of all it is gone all too quickly anyway and secondly what I have in my life is what I am meant to have. I am fully where I am and the lessons of my day are those that I am ripe for learning. Somehow I hold what I have far more dearly when I truly let myself see and feel how temporary it all is. I will cherish my children in my life today while they are here.

**I am passing through
this rich and wonderful world.**

Death borders upon our birth, and our cradle stands in the grave.

Joseph Hall

*T*oday I believe that the buried anxieties and fears that I repress are not "out of sight out of mind." Rather they are very much alive in the unconscious atmosphere in the house. Refusing to acknowledge certain sides of myself does not give them less power but more. It is very confusing to my children to tune in on and feel the feelings I am actually feeling and to be told by me that I am not feeling them. This makes my children wonder if they are the problem and to worry and search for what is wrong with them. In their frantic search they act out with frustration and then they actually look like the problem. If I can handle my own feelings with honesty, my family will have a better chance.

I will keep the focus on myself.

Dress and undress thy soul: mark the decay and growth of it. If, with thy watch, that too be down, then wind up both; since we shall be most surely judged, make the accounts agree.

George Herbert

$\mathcal{T}$oday I understand that my children need to come first much of the time. It is hard to reconcile this with "taking care of myself" which is so important in recovery, but in truth I can often do both. Because I consider them first, it does not mean that I do not consider myself. It only means that I am able to wait a few minutes better than they are. I must and will get back to myself. If I am willing to attend to my child in this conscientious way, the times when I need to put my own needs first will be easier; those times are important. We are a family and we need to compromise. My children will be slowly weaned over the years from needing and getting my immediate attention.

I can set priorities.

Be careful how you live. You may be the only Bible some person ever reads.

William J. Toms

Today I recognize that more than a good time, more than stability, more than happiness, what my children need is *truth*. Life will happen to my children whether I want it to or not. Protecting them from it is an illusion and only confuses things because it's never really clear underneath it all who I really want to protect — them or the still wounded child within me. The truth may hurt for a while but lies and denial will hurt much longer. Children know the truth of the situation unconsciously and it is painful for them when what they know inside is never spoken of or validated.

I can share and live with the truth.

If you add to the truth, you subtract from it.

The Talmud

*T*oday I will trust in God completely as I do everything within my own power to improve my life. I have legs, arms, will, energy and intelligence and I will not waste them. It is really up to me. What I experience in my life is in direct relationship to what I am willing to see and handle. I will not be indolent. When my children look at me they will see someone who is willing to get in there and play. Life is a privilege and I am lucky to be alive. I want to make the most of my time. I don't need to do something the world sees as important to be important. If I live connected to a source of energy and spirituality, the rest will fall into place.

I will use what God gave me.

In God we trust. All others pay cash.

Sign used in retail stores
during the Depression

Today I turn over to a power greater than myself all that is beyond my control. I don't want to postpone being happy until my life is perfect and free from any strife. If I am going to be happy today, I need to let go. My children seem so much freer and self-directed when I am able to give them some space. I am present and available in their lives to provide the security that will make the space feel full and unthreatening, but I am not on top of them. When I don't fret all of the small snags and let them throw me into a panic, we all do better. Life is a different experience altogether when I live it "one day at a time," when I allow it to unfold before me instead of trying to pry open the package before it arrives.

I let go of what is beyond my control.

There is only one way to happiness and that is to cease worrying about things which are beyond the power of our will.

Epictetus

KINDNESS

$\mathcal{T}$oday I understand the deep value of showing kindness to those I love and to people in general. I can get so consumed with my own opinion and limited sense of how the world should be that I forget how little I really see. If I truly saw it all, I would probably have love and patience for just about everyone. Taking care of myself doesn't mean that I should lose track of what it means to care about other people. It is not co-dependent, from a position of love and strength, to extend myself in thoughtful ways to those around me. I am creating my own world — why shouldn't it be pleasant?

I can give for the sake of giving.

It's a bit embarrassing to have been concerned with the human problem all of one's life and find at the end that one has no more to offer by way of advice than "Try to be a little kinder."

Aldous Huxley

Today I let my spirituality be a quiet thing in my life — my own private affair. I don't need to tell anyone how serene I am or have a look of strained contemplation on my face. My spirituality is an everyday thing, as much present while baking cookies and cleaning the kitchen as any other time. My spirituality comes across to my children, not in what I say to them but in how I treat them. Life and spirituality are inseparable, which makes climbing a tree or shopping for a doll house potentially spiritual acts. It is the love, concern and joy with which I participate in these things with my children that make them spiritual. Action is an outgrowth of intention and at some deep level my children sense and internalize my intention.

I see spirituality in everyday things.

Live like a bourgeois, and think like a demigod.

Gustave Flaubert

Today I commit myself to recovery as a path to self-knowledge and spirituality. I needn't stop learning when my storehouse of pain, anger, resentment and grief are cleared out. Life is beautiful and I want to be a part of the mystery. Why live day to day as if all of the profound unknowns of life did not exist, as if all that exists is only what I see? My children remind me of life's mystery. When they come into this world, they are so close to God. They bring me into contact with a sense that there is much more to life than meets the eye. I wonder at what point in life living the illusion becomes more important than living the mystery. My soul is not something that I need to be in eternity to experience; it is with me here right now.

I live in the mystery today.

All men should strive to learn before they die what they are running from and to and why.

James Thurber

Today I am grateful to my children for inspiring me to get the best out of myself. I know that to be the best parent I can be I need to be the best person I can be. There is no such thing as parenting with words and ideas. Children learn what they see — most of parenting is modeling. Because I love my children, I want the person that they model to be worth looking up to. And every day I work to that end. I know that the greatest gift that I can give my children is a happy, healthy, well-adjusted parent who loves them. It is such a deep wish in me not to pass on my family illness of alcoholism and co-dependency to them that it is an extra inspiration to get well.

I appreciate the motivation
my children give me.

Remember, when they have a tantrum, don't have one of your own.

Dr. Judith Kariansky

Today I will walk through this world with my child as my companion. If I am willing to take my child seriously as a person, he will learn to take himself seriously as a person. If I don't minimize what my child says by dismissing it as whimsical or giggling at him when he wants to be heard, he will not minimize himself. I am not so far away from my child's experience that I cannot understand and relate to it. In fact sometimes I identify only too strongly but that can work for the relationship too. We can share a very sacred space together, filled with love, commitment and understanding. I know it is my job to parent my child but that doesn't mean that we can't be friends.

I befriend my child today.

I do not believe in a child world . . . I believe the child should be taught from the very first that the whole world is his world, that adult and child share one world, that all generations are needed.

Pearl S. Buck

*T*oday I greet the world, not only with resolutions of what to achieve, but with a willingness to embrace life as it is. If I miss all that is contained in this moment, then I miss it all. The beauty, purpose and mystery that are always available to me are my real treasures in this world. This year I learn about life and love and simplicity. I want what I pass on to my children to go into their hearts where no one can take it away. I want to know them and I want them to know me.

I am a part of the now.

If you feel that you are lacking in ambition, be assured that meditation and contemplation . . . is a more certain joy in life. Anyone can indulge ambition; only those who have the spirit can revel in passive enjoyment.

Advice from Samuel White
to his son E.B. White

$\mathcal{T}$oday I remind myself again to trust the moment, to let go of the fantasy of what will be. When I live with my mind suspended through time, I give my life away for the idea of a life. Trusting the moment is for me one of my greatest challenges — to release myself into the now and count on life to hold me up, not to drop me through an invisible trap door if I let go, if I am not, for a while, hypervigilant. Trusting the moment also allows me to be with my family. Children are so oriented to the present. If I am not able to join them there, they will experience me as not really being with them, not being there and they may feel that I don't care about them. It's not enough just to "do" for my children, I also need to "be" with them.

I release myself into the now.

Don't forget until too late that the business of life is not business, but living.

B.C. Forbes

Today I have "nothing to do, nowhere to go and no one to be." I will spend time with life today. Some of the activities I do are fun and add to my experience of life, some are necessary and some are a complete waste of my time, but I do them anyway. In this way I rob myself of my own time. When children play, they seem to understand intuitively that life is what is happening now, not what will happen or did happen or might happen. What they experience, they feel fully. They take pleasure, sadness, beauty, horror and comfort in what there is in the moment. They know that the Higher Power is connected to the now.

**I am a part of the moment
and a part of God.**

Let us not go hurrying about and collecting honey, bee-like buzzing here and there but let us open our leaves like a flower and be receptive, budding patiently.

John Keats

*T*oday I will take responsibility for my own behavior. If I behave badly with my children, I will "promptly admit it and make amends." I will make amends for two reasons. The first is to remove the block from my own spiritual path. It's easier to say "I goofed" and move on. The second is to release my children from having to take responsibility for it by rationalizing, hiding, denying or carrying anger — because I won't deal with it they will end up with it in their laps. I also want to ask for their forgiveness, both to clear my own hurt and resentment and theirs. It is a way of giving them their power back if I have abused my power over them.

I can be humble with my children.

Resolve, and thou art free.

Henry Wadsworth Longfellow

Today I will behave in appropriate ways and respect other people's boundaries. In my alcoholic home we felt that whatever happened to one of us happened to all of us. We meddled in each other's most private affairs under the guise of openness and honesty. Rather than understand and take responsibility for our own behavior, it felt safer and smarter to be preoccupied with the behavior of those around us. Openness led to being the target of the collective illness, so we learned to be silent, manipulative and isolated instead. I can live in better ways today.

I remove the log from my own eye.

Should you happen to notice that another person is extremely tall or overweight, eats too much or declines convivial drinks, has red hair or goes about in a wheelchair, ought to get married or ought not to be pregnant — see if you can refrain from bringing these astonishing observations to that person's attention.

Judith Martin, "Miss Manners"

Today I respect what love and kindness can do. There is so much concern today with boundaries, with not caretaking, with meeting one's own needs. All of these things are good and necessary, but not if they push away my ability to love and empathize with others. We sometimes say that ACoAs live as if we are at a rehearsal for life and life itself were going to happen at some later date. My recovery should not become another rehearsal for life. Life is what is happening each day and recovery exists to return me to it, not to take me away from it. My children are a part of my life today. They don't seem to be rehearsing for anything.

I see love and goodness in the world.

True love comes quietly, without banners or flashing lights. If you hear bells, get your ears checked.

Erich Segal

Today I will take time for myself. When I get out of sorts, quick-tempered, short with my children, when life weighs heavily upon me and I think everything is a little wrong, it may only be that I haven't taken any quiet time for a while. When I have enough real solitude to get in touch with a deeper source within me, life seems smoother and I am aware of a kind of beauty and mystery in my day. My children need this too. Instead of worrying that they aren't busy enough and packing their lives with constant activity, I will leave spaces in their day and allow them their moments of quiet.

I turn within for peace.

When from our better selves we have too long been
    parted by the hurrying world, and droop,
Sick of its business, of its pleasures tired.
How gracious, how benign, is Solitude.

William Wordsworth

*T*oday I will wake up to my real life. I am like an adolescent always waiting to make external changes to ward against the overwhelming upheavals that are going on inside of me. I recognize now that these inner wranglings are a part of living on this earth, that change is constant and disquieting. Today I know that I need not be a slave to my own inner workings. I can allow myself some distance from my own process. I am the person who I am most afraid of. My own changeability is more threatening to me than anybody else's. It is up to me to take the attitudes that I want to take; my life is in my own hands.

**I am the master of my
own inner world.**

I am tired of ruling over slaves.

Last words of
Frederick The Great

Today I understand that the world is filled with as much beauty as I am able to perceive. My life is as rich as my inner self can accommodate. My children come by this purity and innocence naturally. They enter life with an excitement and interest that for a long time kept mine alive too. It is, however, up to me to keep the child within me tuned in and alert so that my interest in life does not disappear under layers of mistrust, cynicism and ennui. This is a challenge to my spirit. I will not live forever. What will I gain by going through life as if I had a hundred days for every one that I really have, as if I had all the time in the world to waste?

**I am showing up for what
is good in my life.**

The perception of beauty is a moral test.

Henry David Thoreau

$\mathcal{T}$oday I will remember that the natural order of all things is to be free. If I am learning anything in this road of recovery, it is that an open hand holds things better than a closed one. I can keep nothing that I really want in my life by clutching at it. I cannot keep the best of myself by holding on. It is a constant process of letting go. This is the paradox, that I do a better job of keeping the people and things that I want in my life if I am willing and able to release them. My mate, my close friends and my children are all in this and so am I. I hang on to myself with the same unforgiving grip. I need to loosen up on all of us. I need to recognize this truth that I cannot hold things in my life through hanging on; a tight grip is too much for me and those I love.

I can learn to let go.

A robin redbreast in a cage
Puts all heaven in a rage.

William Blake

Today I recognize not only my fear of being abandoned but also my fear of wanting to abandon myself and what I care about. When people, work or places get in too close, I want to leave them. Originally I felt abandoned and I never want to feel that pain again, so I keep myself at arm's length and am unable to tolerate my own dependency. My "get-out-of-here-quick" switch is easily activated and I become angry at whoever activates it, by not being the way I want them to be — even my children. It's easy when they are little — they need me, it's all very clear. But as they grow older, even they can activate in me this desire to get away. I need to understand in myself not only my fear of being abandoned but also my desire to abandon.

I will not abandon myself.

I know well what I am fleeing from but not what I am in search of.

Michel de Montaigne

Today I will not overprotect my children. The way not to do this is by processing my own pain. If I am clear about my issues, if I have felt the feelings and learned the lessons, I will recognize that pain is a part of growth and self-knowledge. If I cannot face my own pain, I will try to keep my children from pain just as I keep myself from it. If I try to protect my children from what is a natural part of living, they will not develop the emotional muscle they need to cope with life. It is a mistake for me to think that by protecting my children, I am sparing them when actually what I am doing is weakening them. My role is to provide one safe and loving place in this world where they are always welcome and valued.

I provide shelter in the storm.

Common sense is not so common.

Voltaire

Today I see life as an unending adventure. No matter what I have or do not have, no matter how great my success or failure, I never need lose my understanding that life is to be lived, that each day is in fact a new beginning and life is constantly renewing itself. Along with practical knowledge I would like to pass on to my children my spirit of adventure. I am not going to aim my children for one narrow version of success when there is so much more out there to be had. If my children can live with uncertainty, there will be much more of this world available to them. If they have a sense of security and belonging anchored within themselves, they can be certain they are where they are meant to be and spirituality is with them.

I am certain that life is within me.

What is this?

Dying words of Leonard Bernstein

Today I graciously pass on the beauty of
my youth to my children. Life does not
mean for me to be young forever, and if I do
not let youth pass away and die for me, I will
not transform and be reborn into my next
depth. If I hang on to youth, I live in the past
because youth is my past. The paradox is
that when I hang on to youth, I feel old,
whereas if I am willing to let it go, I will have
integrated it and I can move on with youth as
an ever-present part of me. We are every
day being reborn into life. If I subscribe to
the cultural media's idea of what youth is,
not only will I not gain youth, I will lose it.
Why not let my children be young, and I will
explore a different kind of youthfulness.

I will learn who I am.

*Rabbi Zusya said that at the day of judgment, God
would ask him, not why he had not been Moses, but
why he had not been Zusya.*

Walter Kaufmann

Today I recognize my tendency to see things as black and white and get stuck in limited patterns. I realize this comes from living in a dysfunctional household where behaviors became rigid and inflexible. Even "hanging loose" and taking things as they came was in my family an inflexible pattern because no one was able to make plans and follow through. Our rigid patterns were deceptive because sometimes they wore other masks. I know they are rigid patterns because they cannot be adjusted according to the needs of a situation; they are patterns that are superimposed on every situation whether they fit or not, and when I try to change them, I am seen as wrong and out of step. I do not need to repeat this way of operating with my own family if I am willing to change and try something new.

I can change my rigid patterns.

Let thy vices die before thee.

English Proverb

Today I understand the peace there is in quiet. Sometimes my children just want to gaze and take the world in. They absorb it in a way that I rarely do anymore. My memories from my childhood are so active and sensual — the wind on my face, the smell of spring, the sensory experiences of opening my front door, the feel of the house. My ability to take in was so strong, I was so absorbent. My child is building his storehouse of memories each day that we are together. This is his childhood; what he looks around and sees, this home that surrounds him, the feeling in the atmosphere, will all be stored away in his mind and used to fuel his life.

I observe my child taking in his world.

The harvest of a quiet eye.

William Wordsworth

Today I will let my children know what I am really feeling. Rising above being hurt by my children does not necessarily mean that I do not tell them honestly that I do feel hurt. It is better if I am real with them than correct. Correct is such a subjective thing anyway and real will tell them more about who I am as their parent and as a person. It will also give them permission to be real with me. I will need to listen to them if I want them to listen to me. My genuine self is one of the nicest things that I can give to my children; it gives them something to go on, a way to be, a person to model. If I try to be something rather than someone, that is what they will think I expect of them. I have the strength and recovery to be my own person today, available to myself and available to them.

Being who I am is enough.

Make not your sail too big for your ballast.

English Proverb

Today I feel like a visitor in this life; everything seems so temporary. The people I know, the things I do, my family, my children are all so alive and rich, full of a kind of sentimental beauty. There is so much in life that I treasure; little activities that may be humdrum today are somehow beautiful and meaningful simply because they are, they exist, they are what is happening. Life in and of itself has meaning for me, not because anything will come of it or that it was something in the past but because the present moment is life and it is happening as if it were meant to be. Today I realize that being something is somewhat of an illusion. I have always been something and I will always be something. This life I have with my children is so short; the years go by faster than I would ever have thought they could.

I know that life is temporary.

The good life is one inspired by love and guided by knowledge.

Bertrand Russell

Today I recognize that life is my guru. I see in situations opportunities to grow. I look for deeper meaning in little things. Situations in my life are perfectly designed to teach me what I need to learn. I am engaged in a growth process with my child. She is a person who I am meant to learn from and she is meant to learn from me. All situations can be teachers to me if I am open to the lessons. It makes my day seem exciting when I feel I can learn from it. It gives a wondrous sense of purpose to my life to know that I never stop learning and growing.

Life is my powerful teacher.

Fortunately analysis is not the only way to resolve inner conflicts. Life itself still remains a very effective therapist.

Karen Horney

Today I recognize that one of the characteristics of co-dependency is feeling other people's feelings for them, rather than feeling my own and letting them feel their own, including my children. This complicates my life very much because I lose track of who feels what. I get a lot of information about myself through my feelings and I get information about other people by observing how they feel. When I feel other people's feelings for them, I don't get information about either of us. To be able to put myself in another person's place, feel what they might be feeling and then return to myself is helpful; to feel their feelings instead of mine is confusing and painful. One way to feel my own feelings is to take responsibility for them. If I am in denial about my own feelings, I will not be able to center myself and grow personally.

Good or bad, this is what I feel.

Children are unpredictable. You never know what inconsistency they're going to catch you in next.

Franklin P. Jones

I recognize that in dealing with my child there are many places along the way where I can get hooked in with issues from my own past. I need to separate my own past from what is going on with my child in the present. Is the pain from my own childhood or is it really pain from today's interaction with my child? One way to keep our identities separate is for me to really look at who I am today and where I came from with a measure of honesty and objectivity. If I need to rewrite the past, I will also try to rewrite the present. My freedom and my child's freedom will be not in seeing things as I want them to be, but in accepting my past as it was and my present as it is.

I see things as they are.

We cannot defend freedom abroad by deserting it at home.

Edward R. Murrow

Today I recognize that my child needs to learn not so much to be done for but to do for himself. The more my child can do for himself, the better his self-image will be. I will help my child to walk through fear and frustration and teach him that these feelings are a part of life that everyone experiences. I want my child to feel good about himself and to feel that he can take care of himself. It will take me longer to teach my child than to just do for him, but it will be worth it in the long run. The quickest way to become an expert is to learn to be a beginner and I will teach my child that life is full of being a beginner — that it is okay not to know.

I will patiently teach my child.

Give a man a fish and you feed him for a day.
Teach a man to fish and you feed him for a lifetime.

Chinese Proverb

I will not point to a vague and invisible future for my child but will live with him fully in the present. Children build self-confidence by doing and mastering in the now. They need to learn to be independent and competent. They need help dealing with situations, finding ways of placing themselves comfortably in the world and living there. When I talk to my child, I will be practical and straight with him and give him tools rather than advice. If I have the broader view in mind as a parent, then I will break it down into usable material that my child can handle today. I will move one step at a time to a larger goal; I will make it easier.

I meet my child on his level of ability.

Never show a child what he cannot see . . . [W]hile you are thinking about what will be useful to him when he is older, talk to him of what he can use now.

Jean-Jacques Rousseau

Today I remind myself that childhood is a time of wonder and magic. Children's minds do not work as adult minds work. They are magical in their thinking and often feel that anything can happen. While on the one hand this magical thinking fills their world and mine with a sense of endless possibility and excitement, it can also produce deep feelings of danger and fear. I will not abandon my children. If I do, they will not know where I have gone or how to get me back. They may even feel, through their identification with me, that they also are gone — that we have both disappeared in some unexplainable way.

I will hang in there with my children.

*Will there really be a morning? Is there such a
    thing as day?
Could I see it from the mountains? If I were as tall
    as they?
Does it feel like water lilies? Has it feathers like a
    bird?
Is it brought from famous countries? Of which I've
    never heard?*

Emily Dickinson

Today I recognize that life is eternal. There is a part of me that is, was and always will be. To contact that part of me is the secret to life eternal. The kingdom of heaven is within me, within my own self and soul and this is the greatest lesson that I can teach my child — to look within, to always keep one eye open within and one open without. If I teach my child how to do everything else besides this and I ignore this deepest truth, what good will I do him? If I teach him to look always outside for happiness, I am training him to be co-dependent.

I teach my child to contact his own soul and inner self.

The voice of Nature loudly cries,
And many a message from the skies,
That something in us never dies.

Robert Burns

I will not train my child to think that what is in her hand is more important than what is in her heart. She can be as accomplished as she chooses and value the things of the world, that is natural, but she needs to first value herself. I will show her how by the way I treat her and treat myself. I will not skip over either of us in a rush to acquire and achieve. I will not leave us behind on our road toward personal fulfillment because if we fulfill our desires but leave ourselves, there will be no one there to enjoy any of these accomplishments. The person who lives deep within me is the seer and the knower — I will not let this person get lost in the shuffle.

I will keep my values straight.

Keep your treasures in heaven, for where your treasures are there shall your heart be also.

The Bible

Today I recognize that in my disease of co-dependency I feel other people's feelings for them. This gets me into trouble because not only are they my perception of their feelings and not necessarily their own, but after a while, I get my feelings confused with theirs. Other people are not necessarily aware they themselves have the feelings I assign them. The crux of the issue is that I am not anyone else but me. I can only do something about my own feelings; when I experience other people's, I feel frustrated because I am unable to change them. Empathy is a beautiful thing; fusing is not a good idea. This is deeply important in raising my children. They need space to feel their own feelings without the burden of mine on top of them.

**I feel my own feelings and let
other people feel theirs.**

Generous people are rarely mentally ill people.

Karl Menninger

Today I am willing to give myself time to go through the full cycle of healing. First a repressed feeling works its way to the surface and I become conscious of its presence. Next I feel it. I feel it in a variety of ways, sometimes with a blast of strong emotion, or it may take over my whole body and fill me with agitation and fear. I may carry it in my body as tension, tightness, headaches or stomachaches. It may be difficult to know just what I am feeling or the feelings may be so strong that I hardly know where they are coming from. I will stay with them and let the feelings pass through, knowing that they are better out of me. When the feelings have moved through, I will feel a little more free, a little more whole.

**I can feel my old feelings rather
than act them out or pass them on.**

Better a tooth out than always aching.

                                        Thomas Fuller

Who I am today is intricately connected with my past. All of the attitudes, activities, people, places and things of my young life played important roles and had a profound impact on forming me. Today I will assess the life that I am creating for my child. What will be the pictures in her mental scrapbook? What, by my own attitude, am I teaching her about life? What is the feeling atmosphere in our home? How do we handle conflict and what does that say to her? Will she think of home as a place where she is loved and accepted no matter what? Will she recall it as a comfortable and sane place? What is my attitude toward life? I am affecting my child's future by how I act today.

**I look at our life and home with
honest eyes and heart.**

Everyone is the child of his past.

Edna G. Rostow

Today I will let the holiday spirit move in and out of me, neither attempting to hold on to it and pump it up nor resisting feeling joy if and when it should come. Rituals in a pain-filled home are filled with silent hurts. I can let that go. I don't have to repeat and repeat and repeat this cycle of pain. When I feel myself getting stuck in old feelings, I will shift my gaze. I will be aware of the feelings and watch them, neither judging nor getting lost in them. I have a right to them but they do not have a right to me. I will feel peace today. I will let the strength of my recovery prevail. I have worked hard to be where I am. Today I will be there fully, without self-consciousness, without apology.

I am my own person.

Do well and you will have no need for ancestors.

Voltaire

I will not ask my children to finish my unfinished business for me. The dreams and hopes I have not lived out are mine to reckon with. My children have their own dreams. They will not be happy doing what they are not meant to do; they will always wonder how they got there. I will let them "follow their own bliss." I will pay attention to what they want to do with their lives and assist them in any way that I can. One of the biggest ways I can help them is to get out of their way and let the energy of their youth and desire propel them. Today I will take responsibility for living out my own dreams and let them have theirs.

I will live each day that I have.

That vague, crepuscular time, the time of regrets that resemble hopes, of hopes that resemble regrets, when youth has passed, but old age has not yet arrived.

Ivan Sergeyevich Turgenev

Today I will treat my children as I wish to be treated and I will behave toward them the way I would like to see them behave in the world. Some of what my children do is just being who they are and part of childhood. Some is a reflection of what they model from me. I remind myself that my actions speak much louder than my words and whatever I do, they will feel they have my permission to do themselves. Children learn by watching and doing. I will pay attention to what I say to them and the message I send to them by how I act. I can teach them more about how to behave by actually behaving that way myself than by talking to them about it. I will take responsibility for my behavior, knowing that it is what I am setting as an acceptable standard for my child.

I observe my own actions.

The loveliest fairy in the world; and her name is Mrs. Doasyouwouldbedoneby.

Charles Kingsley

Today I admire my child's ability to try and fail and try again. What a free period in life not to see trials as failures. I will remember that what I expose my child to at this age he will learn in a wonderful way. I am not going to educate him in a sense of failure by criticizing or pointing out his weak spots. Self-consciousness will crowd out his sense of spontaneity in learning soon enough. For now I admire my child's freedom to fail and I learn from it. If I take that same jolly attitude to my own life, wouldn't we both be better off than if I get him to adopt mine? In this area my child is the teacher and I am the student. I will observe and take into myself his lightheartedness and sense of self-abandon. His excitement to learn and know is inspiring to me.

I learn from my child.

To dry one's eyes and laugh at a fall, and baffled, get up and begin again.

Robert Browning

318

Today I center myself in my own heart and know that it is from here that I can see the farthest. Within the seat of my heart I can rest in an awareness that is not available to my eye. My heart is not just my feelings but a port of entry for a kind of information that goes beyond the five senses; it synthesizes what I take in along with what I know. My heart is stronger than my head and when I am willing to trust in and feel its presence within me, I feel strong and centered in myself. It is easier to begin with my heart and let my head follow than to begin with my head and ask my heart to come along.

I will center my awareness in my heart and feel its presence.

A good heart is better than all the heads in the world.

Edward Bulwer Lytton

Today I will relax and detach myself when my children move through their feelings. Everybody needs space for changing moods and if our home is basically healthy, it can accommodate normal swings. In the home I grew up in, mood swings were serious business — they could turn the whole house upside down for hours or even days. I have carried that fear and habit into my home. I can lose track of whose mood is swinging and soon I can't tell if it's mine or someone else's. This is part of my "disease of attitudes." Today I can tolerate mood changes in myself or my family members and know that they are normal and natural.

It is natural for moods to change.

Love him (or her) and let her (or him) alone. Let him enjoy his troubled moments. He may need an occasional withdrawal or self-inquiry. Don't intrude upon the private mood. It does not necessarily mean he hates you or resents his mother or should be carried off to a couch.

Leo C. Rosten

Today I recognize the angels in my life. I did not get where I am without help; there were people along the way who saw my need and reached out a hand to me. They not only looked and saw but took action and helped me to get my life on track. Today I say a silent prayer of thanks for the presence of these people in my life and I pray for their health and well-being wherever they are. They are people who gave me strength and hope and held me up when I stumbled. I am a better person for what they gave me. I am in a better position to be strong and whole for my children because of the love I have received from them. Perhaps I can pass this on to others.

I say a prayer of thanks for my angels.

Good fortune is God among men, and more than a God.

Aeschylus

Today I wish to see things differently. As I move through my day I watch myself look at a situation one way. If I feel snagged or stuck in my perception, I will quietly say to myself, "I wish to see this differently," and trust that my sincere desire will move me along. I will watch as new ways of seeing a situation present themselves. It is a negative habit to see things as black and white or right and wrong. Today I understand that what appears to be a subtle change can actually create a meaningful and deep shift in awareness. I will attempt to allow my insides to transform my view of the outside. I will look at my children today with fresh new eyes — not as people about whom I know everything, but open to learning something new.

I wish to see things differently.

The foolish and the dead never change their opinions.

James Russell Lowell

Today I realize that what my children need is truth. Protecting them from themselves doesn't work. Protecting them from me is an illusion because they will know at some level what is going on. If I feel one way and act another, they will get conflicting messages and wonder if something is wrong with them. If I feel one thing but say another, they will feel upset because they can't sort out the truth. I can find ways of sharing honestly with my children that are appropriate. First, I will work through my own difficult feelings so I can handle them and they will not color my presentation. Then I will be open with my children.

I offer truth to my children.

If there's a choice between talking and not talking, always choose talking, even if it's more difficult.

Grace Hechinger

Today I will not lie to my children and tell myself that it is for their own good. My children know what's going on; they are curious about everything. It is valuable life-training for them when I explain things thoroughly, making use of their open minds and their ability to learn and absorb information easily when they are young. Life is full of lessons that my children and I can tease out and look at together. This is how they will learn to think, by not being put off but included and talked to. My children are much more likely to value my opinion if I value theirs. We can learn and grow together.

**I share my experience, strength and
hope with my children.**

*It is a great mistake, I think, to put children off
with falsehoods and nonsense, when their growing
powers of observation and discrimination excite in
them a desire to know about things.*

Annie Sullivan

Today I will give my children what will sustain them best — faith in life, in love, in a Higher Power. I will not only teach this with words but by my actions. When I say I will do something, I will follow through. I will run an orderly household where things happen in a way that my children can count on. I will teach them through my actions that it is all right to trust in those around them, that they themselves matter, that it is not foolish to have faith. My trustworthy actions as a parent help my child to build a foundation and a way of seeing life. I will show my children how their Higher Power loves them by the way I love them. I will teach them that it is safe to have faith.

——

I understand that my actions are formative.

Give spiritual strength to people and they will give genuine affection to you.

Anonymous

*T*oday I make choices. Raising children is a long and sometimes overwhelming job. I will let myself flow with it, knowing that just when I get used to something as it is, it will probably change. If I take a broader view of things, it will help me to weather these changes without being constantly thrown off my own track. If I can deal with my own co-dependent inclination to over-identify with my children and under-identify with myself, I will be better able to let things happen, knowing that change is the nature of life. Every time there is a bit of chaos in my life I do not need to swing into action myself. If I let things happen as they are meant to, a lot of my work will be done for me and much strain will be removed from my life.

**I can flow with my parenting
and with life.**

Learn not to sweat the small stuff.

Kenneth Greenspan

Today I can tolerate love and kindness. I built a wall around my heart as a child to protect myself from being hurt. I pretended to myself that I was independent and didn't need people to be interested in me. I acted as if my parents' indifference to my life didn't really matter. They were not aware of the details of my life and so I thought that my life was unimportant. I didn't let on how deeply abandoned and unloved I felt. I could let people be kind to me from a distance but if they got too close, it only hurt. I felt that if I let them in they would only leave me. Today I allow for the possibility in my life of healthy, fulfilling relationships. Today I am in control of much that, as a child, I had to just live with.

I take action when I hurt to get reassurance.

We should feel sorrow, but not sink under its oppression. The heart of a wise man should resemble a mirror, which reflects every object without being sullied by any.

Confucius

Today I recognize that my children live in a world of their own. I will not cordon off my children's world so that it includes only their own age group. I recognize their need to interact with all sorts of people and to forge bonds for themselves. How will my children learn to interact with the world if I keep them away from it? Even with the best of intentions a limited world is a limited world. I don't want to teach my children how to isolate themselves either by class, race or philosophy. They will develop inner strength if they feel that they can negotiate a wide variety of situations.

I will expose my children to a larger world.

Life was meant to be lived, and curiosity must be kept alive. One must never, for whatever reason, turn his back on life.

Eleanor Roosevelt

Today I honor my deep search for recovery. Not everyone would put themselves through what I am putting myself through in order to recover and get well. They would see themselves as fine and me as having a problem. Today I do not judge them for judging me. I have made a commitment to recovery because I believe in it, because I see with my eyes and heart that it is better to be than not to be. This is the gift that I am giving myself and my children little by little, one day at a time. This is the legacy that I want to leave.

I am proud to be committed to recovery.

I seem to have been only like a boy playing on the seashore, and diverting myself in now and then finding a smoother pebble or a prettier shell than ordinary, whilst the great ocean of truth lay all undiscovered before me.

Sir Isaac Newton

Today I resolve to live my life close to my own insides. What good will it do me if I chase someone else's dream? I have dreams of my own and desires that are important to me. I don't want to fill my days with a thousand half-truths. I have a right to be who I am and my children have a right to be who they are. I don't want to systematically remove them from themselves by asking them to be what is not them. They can learn to be socialized without giving themselves over to an idea of who they are supposed to be. First I will reinforce and affirm them, then I will give them direction; first I will help them to build a self and then direct it. I don't want to make my children conform to an image that will ultimately remove them from themselves or create an external voice that drowns out their own internal voice.

I affirm my children for who they are.

For God's sake, choose a self and stand by it!

William James

Today I understand that it is not good for me or my children if I let them take things out on me. Growing up in a dysfunctional home I felt that my parents' problems were my problems and that I inherited their pain. Inheritance can travel upwards also. My children's problems should not be mine — in either direction there is a boundary problem. The antidote to being abused by my parents is not to be abused by my children. Because I am used to considering myself to be the problem, it is possible that I will also train my children to see me as the problem. I need to learn what abuse is and learn not to accept it from anyone. If this is going to work, I also need to not abuse anyone else. When I behave in abusive ways to my children, I will stop myself. The cycle of abuse is just that, a cycle, and it needs to stop at all points.

I am willing to be healthy.

Accustom children to a true notion of things.

George Shelley

*T*oday I will allow myself to really experience my fears. I always remain on the
outside of them, doing a mad dance to keep
from feeling them. Recovery has taught me
to surrender. If I am afraid, I will let myself
be afraid and see where that feeling leads
me. I will go into the feeling when I am in a
safe place to do it, when my children are not
in my charge. When I allow myself to feel
my feelings, they have a way of expanding
my consciousness. I am not carrying on an
inner fight with them in an attempt to get
rid of them and not feel them. The best way
not to have my feelings run me is not to
beat them down but to give them space,
knowing that part of me remains detached
and steady while I give myself the time and
space I need.

I allow myself to feel my painful feelings.

Feelings aren't facts.

12-Step Programs

Today I realize that I am not my job, my past, my clothes or my socio-economic status. When I think along these lines, I mistake the objects I own for myself. If my car gets dented, I will think that I am dented. This is false identification or seeing myself as existing within the things that I own rather than the things that I am. The growth of my mind, soul and spirit can never be taken away from me. What I have developed within me is more lasting and real than the trinkets I gather. I will catch myself today if I give who I am away to what I have, and I will gently remind myself of my true nature. I am one with my Higher Power and eternal truth. I am not the things that I own, just as I am not my children. They belong to themselves and their own Higher Power.

I remain centered in my real self.

*You must look into people as
well as at them.*

Philip D. Stanhope,
Earl of Chesterfield

Today I honor the person with whom I made my children. We are separate individuals. We do or don't get along; sometimes we are perfect, sometimes not at all. But we have done something magnificent together. The love and devotion that we have felt for one another has been put together in these little beings. If my children are a gift from God, then so is the person with whom I made them. Why not learn to love this person unconditionally — the same as I do my children? The love and respect that we show each other creates the context in which our children see relationships and what is possible for them.

**I fully respect the other parent
of my children.**

*Give your hearts, but not into each other's keeping.
    For only the hand of
Life can contain your hearts. And stand together
    yet not too near together.
For the pillars of the temple stand apart, and the
    oak tree and the cypress grow not in each other's
    shadow.*

Kahlil Gibran

$\mathcal{T}$oday I pass on an attitude of beauty to my children. I will freely tell them how wonderful I think they are, knowing that their parents' words are big and important to them. These messages will go into their subconscious and help to create an attitude they will take toward themselves. My positive reflection of them will become their positive self-reflection of themselves. All of the seemingly insignificant little words of praise or affection I tell them will go into forming a quiet inner voice that will speak softly in their own minds. Many of my child's "super ego" voices that speak loudly within his mind are the things I say to him now and he takes into his mind as his own.

I will tell you how wonderful you are.

If you carry yourself like a beauty, people will think of you as one.

Mother's advice quoted by
Michele Slung

I can set limits today for my child. When I was young, I felt overwhelmed and out of control. The anger and underlying sense of violence in my home scared me and I withdrew to protect myself. Now when my children express anger, it frightens me and I withdraw. That place of fear and powerlessness gets activated and I become an anxious child myself. When this happens, rather than parent my children by setting limits on their behavior, I give in because I am scared and overwhelmed myself. This is not good parenting and all I am teaching them is that they will get what they want if they press hard enough. Today I am willing to feel the feelings that rage and anger induced in me as a child so that I can work through them and learn to set the limits my children need.

I can feel my own feelings and set limits for my child.

The past just came up and kicked me.

Vanessa Williams

Today I will not ignore my inner reality in favor of an idea of reality. What is true for me is who I am and where and how I stand. I will not ask my child not to know what he knows. Children are deeply conscious beings and pick up much more than we dare to imagine. Because their intellects are so undeveloped, they don't edit and block emotional information the way we do later in life. If when they confront me with how they feel, I brush them away and treat them as if their reality is somehow wrong or unimportant, they will feel out of sync and discounted. My children deserve to be heard by me, whatever their point of view.

I will honor my child's point of view.

The sooner you treat your son as a man, the sooner he will be one.

John Dryden

Today I understand that my child has an inner source of quiet. If I allow my child to work or play undisturbed by me until he is fully spent, his next period of concentrated activity will be very likely deeper and longer. Children have their own inner tempo and I will respect that of my child's. I notice that when I require my child to change his activity without warning, he seems jarred and upset. Perhaps this is because he is in his own deep cycle of work and my action comes as an interruption to his personal pace. Much is going on that I cannot see; my child may lack age but he does not lack depth.

I will allow my child his own pace.

Respect the child. Be not too much his parent. Trespass not on his solitude.

Ralph Waldo Emerson

Today I deepen and grow in my understanding of myself. I am no longer trying to silence painful voices within me with expressions like, "Keep a stiff upper lip" or, "When the going gets tough, the tough get going . . ." They are good sayings for life as it happens, but I am on a path of recovery and recovery is not about toughing things out. Recovery is a path of self-discovery. When I learn to see and hear what is really going on with me, I will not hide things from myself. I can then learn to understand how they affect my relationships today.

I am ready to look inside.

You have not converted a man because you have silenced him.

John, Viscount Morley
of Blackburn

Today I need not be so caught up in recovery that I think every feeling I have has to be spoken, resolved or worked through. Repression was a part of my disease but that doesn't mean that health means letting anything or everything out. Recovery gives me the ability to choose. Some things need to be addressed, some shelved or filed for later, some just witnessed impartially and released. Much of what my children want from me is a nonjudgmental listener. My impulse to take action all the time inhibits their comfort in simply sharing their feelings with me. I need to learn to simply be with my own feelings and theirs and then let them go.

**I can be a good listening friend
to myself and my child.**

Think like a man of action, act like a man of thought.

Henri Bergson

Today I accept my path of recovery as the beginning of a new life lived in harmony with the universe. It is not only to heal past wounds that I work this path but to release my spirit. I am not looking backward and wallowing in old pain. The strong way is not the way of self-denial and repression. I am taking the strong way by willingly visiting my past pain once and for all with awareness and understanding so that it can stop visiting me. I can run away from anything but myself. My children will inherit my possessions, money and valuables. They will also inherit my pain. What I do not resolve within myself, the pain and anger that I carry around in silence, is heard and felt by them. Today because I love them I will work on myself.

I am on a path toward my spiritual self.

The surest way into the Universe is through a forest wilderness.

John Muir

*T*oday I will attempt a *Leap of Faith* and accept that what I would like to see in my life can happen for me. I will direct my life from the inside towards the outside rather than the reverse. I am not just a responder to what goes on around me. It is the way in which I respond that speaks to who I am. In choosing my response I define my reality. Life no longer has to prove itself to me for me to think it is worthy of my love. I love life the way it is — for its own sake. I observe that when I experience change in my life it seems to follow, however subtly, some shift in attitude or a willingness to allow change to happen. I have seen the power my own thoughts have in my life.

I am willing to believe my life can feel full and abundant.

Some things have to be believed to be seen.

Ralph Hodgson

SKEPTICISM AND VULNERABILITY *December 8*

Today I will not seek to protect myself from feeling vulnerable by hiding under a cynical tough exterior. When my child shrugs his shoulders, hardens his face and says "I don't care," "It doesn't bother me," I will take a second look to make sure that he is not hiding his real feelings in fear of appearing vulnerable. I needn't quiz him and invade his privacy by insisting that he is not being fully open but I will take note in my own mind that he may be experiencing some inner pain. And if it keeps repeating itself, I will do a little gentle investigating or just give him a pep talk with words of encouragement. Maybe I'll just sit beside him and quietly let him know how much he means to me.

**I will keep my eyes open and
my ear to the ground.**

Skepticism is a hedge against vulnerability.

Charles Thomas Samuels

*T*oday I will carve out peaceful time to focus on myself. It is easy to take care of myself when I am sick or in crisis; then I feel justified in asking for attention and giving myself a break. In recovery, I learn to focus on and take care of myself when I feel good because it feels good. It is natural to like to enjoy myself and it is my responsibility to be good to me. When I know how to do that, I see my children differently. I am able to encourage them to respond to their own needs and support their enjoying their own lives without jealousy.

**I am able to parent myself
and my children.**

A stitch in time saves nine.

Old Proverb

Today I will accept that my child is sent forth into this world from me — from the home that I create, from the atmosphere that I set down. It is an awesome responsibility to be a parent but a responsibility that I wish to be on friendly terms with. When I accept its magnitude and understand that all I can do is my best, I can break it down. Being a parent is not the only role I play in life and I will not serve myself or my children by making it my only role. I will seek balance in my life and model that for my children. I will show them in meaningful ways that I am there for them and for myself as well.

I am a person and a parent.

You are the bows from which your children as living arrows are sent forth.

Kahlil Gibran

Today I take in what my children say and do. I think about it, reflect on it and allow what they put out to play in the shadows of my mind. I let my mind reflect a while on various images of them before I act on or judge what they are saying and doing. When I react too quickly to my children, I sometimes overpower them and stop their flow of sharing themselves with me. A lot of times all that they want is a loving audience — someone who cares about them just to listen and they go away feeling heard, feeling relieved, feeling held.

I can do a lot by doing less.

Mirrors should reflect a little before throwing back images.

Jean Cocteau

*T*oday I am grateful for the gentleness of you — the quiet way in which you enter my soul and sail on a mythical journey through the waters of my heart and mind. Oh, little you. How ever did you come into my life? Though I remember all of the physical realities of your coming as if they were printed in time, it still seems you came as if by magic, the answer to a quiet dream, the reaching out of my innermost self into the ether where you must have been waiting. There is more poetry in the turn of your head, the stretching of your hand and limb than in all the volumes that I know. How lucky I feel to know your presence in my life.

I thank God for you.

nobody, not even the rain, has such small hands

e e cummings

Today I will do more than pass on knowledge to my child; I will pass on self-understanding. All of the information in the world cannot bring my child closer to his own truth if I ask him in a thousand little ways to turn away from it. When he talks, I will listen and when he tells me how he feels, I will accept that as true for him. We can discuss things and come to new awarenesses and understandings but first he needs to feel validated where he is. I want my child to have a sense of what he likes and dislikes so that he can make choices for himself in life that will suit his nature. He is not wrong if he disagrees with my ideas — only different. I will let him be himself.

I will raise a choicemaker.

In search of my mother's garden, I found my own.

Alice Walker

Today I will realize that communication is all-important. My child and I are two different people and the only way we will get to know each other is by learning to really listen and really share honestly. We need to give of ourselves in each of these ways to know one another. As a parent I tend to feel that I know my child through and through. I need to remember that no one knows anyone else's insides. I may not have learned how to talk with considerate honesty and listen with the same attitude, but I can learn if I am willing to check my own reactiveness and be thoughtfully honest. In this way we will come to know one another.

I would like to get to know you.

What we've got here is a failure to communicate.

Donn Pearce

*T*oday I feel a deep respect for life and all that this world and this force provide for me. There is more beauty and variety in this world than I can possibly take in and the deep spiritual truth that I search all over for is somehow coded into all that is alive. Being a spiritual person is largely a recognition that what I am made of, what this world and all life is made of is already of the spirit. It is not a matter of working for something but of realizing what already is. Somehow babies and little children know this. What they feel, they feel; what they are, they are.

I am able to take in the beauty of life and see its many gifts.

Late on the third day, at the very moment when, at sunset . . . there flashed upon my mind unforeseen and unsought, the phrase, Reverence for Life . . .

Albert Schweitzer

Today I hear the voice that my child speaks with alongside the voice of my own inner child. Each of us has a child within us and each of us needs to feel heard and expressive. It is the child inside of me who gets excited over projects and people and life; it is through my inner child that I experience my greatest and most simple sense of self because the child in me came first. When I look at my own child, I will see an adult in the making — an adult who will have a strong and healthy child alive inside. I will let the child inside of me out to play with my children; we can have a good time together.

I honor the child within us both.

Only when I make room for the voice of the child within, do I feel myself to be genuine and creative.

Alice Miller

Today when my child hangs his head and finds it hard to communicate his feelings to me, rather than see it as a rejection of my attempts to help, I will recognize that what he needs is love and patience. Children aren't born knowing how to verbalize their needs; they have to learn this and it's not easy. If I can teach my child to understand his own feelings and be willing to share them, he will be much better able to live a happy life. This is easier said than done. Educating others to reflect on their own process is no small thing. It will also require that I am willing to reflect on mine and I know how difficult that can be. If I can count to ten and show some patience, then maybe I can ask my child to do the same. Today I will try.

I will learn patience and teach patience.

Look at the humans on this planet as either extending love or as fearful and sending out a call for love.

Gerald Jampolsky

Today I remember the value of taking life easy and living one day at a time. I want to know the outcome so I can finally relax and enjoy the in-between, forgetting that life is the in-between. Goals are meant to give us focus and outcomes are the fruits of labor, but life is what happens along the way. If I need to know who my children will be to love them as they are, I will lose them. I simply cannot exist anywhere but this point in time. To try to do anything else is to re-move myself from my own experience of life. Children tend to be very focused in the present. I will observe them and see how they operate rather than pull them out into my anxiety.

I recognize my inclination to race ahead.

Easy Does It.

12-Step Saying

Today I admire the sense of purpose with which my children move through their day. They don't seem to second-guess themselves and each of their activities takes on an air of importance that I cannot help but notice. So much that I have come to take for granted is born again in their hands and under their gaze. They are wholly unambivalent. They bring to bear all of their creative energies and talents to a task that makes it appear as if it had never been attempted before. I don't know what place inside themselves they operate from, but my children are always determined to know what they are about and where they are going. To interrupt them would seem to trespass on their very selves.

**I stand back and watch my children
with respect.**

I had seen a herd of elephants traveling through dense native forest . . . pacing along as if they had an appointment at the end of the world.

Isak Dinesen (Karen Blixen)

Today I will not pretend to my children that I am not searching for my identity just as they are. Nor will I pretend that growing up solves the question, "Who am I?" I will only share with them the truth, how the question changes as I grow older. Life is never quiet, and although I am content, I am not satisfied. I will always be looking, yearning, wishing to know the unknowable. As I look back on my own parents, my most cherished moments are not when they told me their answers but when they entrusted me with their questions, when for treasured moments we explored together and opened our soul's searchings to one another.

I allow myself to show.

"Then you are thirsty, too?" I demanded.

Antoine de Saint Exupery

Today I make my own rules. It's tempting to conduct my life, parenting and gauge expectations of my child so that they match up to what I perceive to be the going, acceptable thing. We have, however, our own unique personalities. Life is really the clinic. Each situation that is presented to us offers an opportunity for growth. I have my own style of learning and my own learning curve. So does my child. If we try to fit our growth to other people's, we will end up living out their thoughts and ideas. We have our own thoughts and ideas. What would be so wrong with a life tailored to fit us? The same goes for my children — they are unique.

Make rules — break rules.

If a man does not keep pace with his companions, perhaps it is because he hears a different drummer. Let him step to the music which he hears, however measured or far away.

Henry David Thoreau

I will be on time today. Part of creating a secure home for my children is to respect their lives by respecting their schedule. Being there does not only mean emotional presence; it has a very practical side too. When our lives happen on schedule, my children learn that they can count on things — that they can trust. When children are left for hours, they feel forgotten and abandoned. When I say I will be there, I will be there or I will call to explain why I am not and reschedule. Thirty minutes may not seem like much to me but that can feel like hours to my children. I will not take advantage of their dependency on me and create in them a confusion of loyalties between their needs and my actions.

I will respect my child's schedule.

Never reach out your hand unless you're willing to extend an arm.

Elizabeth Fuller

Today I recognize that being there for my child takes many forms. I will remember holidays and do little things that let them know I care. If I find that I am forgetting things that I know matter to them like Valentine's Day, friends' names or important facts in their lives, I will ask myself what is going on with me. What am I telling them by forgetting these things? What am I not seeing in my own feelings? Do I fear getting excited about holidays because they were disappointing and painful to me as a child? Do I forget things and keep myself in an intentional fog to defend myself from counting on things too much and then being let down?

I will examine my reactions.

The mill cannot grind with water that's past.

George Herbert

The home I create for my children gives them a place to be — a place to be inside of themselves and a place to be in the world. I remember what it was like to feel that I had my own special position in my family, that I was loved and valued, that my presence was important. Disease took that place away from me. I wanted to avoid feeling the pain I felt at losing that first precious feeling of being loved and belonging — when I had parents, when I had brothers and sisters, when I belonged somewhere. Today I know that feeling those feelings is the only way to get out of them and to release the control they have over me. I will know what I lost so that I can know what I can have again and give.

**I cherish my place and create
one for my children.**

*Because I remember I despair. Because I remember
I have the duty to reject despair.*

Elie Wiesel

Today I see that the distance I can stretch my arm out in all directions is the area I can do something about. I can change the world by changing myself. I can live a conscious life. As a parent I can make a difference by loving my children — by sending them into their day full inside. If they feel loved, that is what they will share with those around them. All the ideas and philosophies in this world are just so many words without the human touch. Touching and being touched is what we really have. I recognize that love and Higher Power happen through me. I am the divine conduit for the energy of life.

I will really feel and share life and love.

and if ever i touched a life i hope that life knows that i know that touching was and still is and always will be the true revolution.

nikki giovanni

Today I recognize that I treat myself the way I was treated. How my parents behaved toward me taught me step by step how to act toward myself. Where they were patient with me, I tend to be patient with myself. Where they were hard on me, I tend to be hard on myself. I recreate my past truth in the present day. The way I treat my child today will be the way he will treat himself tomorrow. If I act consciously and with kindness, love and intelligent direction toward him, he has a much better chance of living out these qualities. If I accept him and love him as he is, won't he naturally learn to do this for himself? I have a great impact on my child's future by how I treat him today.

**I will behave consciously toward
my children.**

A person is a person because he recognizes others as persons.

Bishop Desmond Tutu

*T*oday when someone makes me angry I can tell them about it. I never knew that was possible. I thought I had to act out anger in order to express it. I had no idea that in acting it out, I feel less of the real feeling than if I simply let myself experience my anger as my own emotion. Once I do this, I really know that I am angry about something and I can do something about it. I can talk it over with others without blasting them off the map. When I blast my anger, the cause is lost because the person whom I am angry with gets upset and defensive. When I don't acknowledge my anger at all, I become passive-aggressive, speaking and delivering quiet hurts in covert ways like withdrawing love or ignoring someone else's feelings. That can hurt as much or more than being blasted. When I feel my anger, I take responsibility for it as *my* feeling.

I am responsible for my own anger.

Promote yourself but do not demote another.

Israel Salanter

Today I recognize how fearful I can be at the thought of having a family of my own. Family was something I ran from, something that caused me pain and which I grew to mistrust. Unfortunately I bring those feelings of fear and mistrust to my own family today. Somewhere deep inside of me I can't really believe that this could work out — that we won't become another loving family turned sour like mine did. But I can't cover over my fears any longer. When I do, they have a way of controlling me and leaking out the edges. In anticipation of an eruption I help to create one, or in fear of things not working out, I abandon my family or spouse to protect myself against being abandoned. Today I will be willing to feel my deep fear of having a happy family.

I give my fears space and respect.

There is only one way to happiness and that is to cease worrying about things which are beyond the power of our will.

Epictetus

Today I accept that my children will grow up. I experience the growing up and going away of my children as a kind of death of my little family — which it is. But this is a healthy loss that will give way to new exciting possibilities if I can let it happen. Hanging on will only prolong my own agony and everyone else's. It also may have serious, destructive effects on my children because they will have one foot in their own lives and one foot in mine, taking care of me. It may look as if they need me but isn't it really the other way around perhaps? My fear of abandonment and previous losses makes me hurt to have my family growing up.

I can let go.

You have to let your children go if you want to keep them.

Malcolm Forbes

I am not raising my child so that she can prove to me that she is completely put together. There will be unevenness in growth, jagged edges, areas that need work and attention, but today I know that the finished product is an illusion. My child will change and grow all of her life and my job is not to finish her off but to begin her well — to lay a foundation upon which a person can be built; to help her to recognize and develop those qualities within herself that are unique and hers to develop; to help her to know her gifts; to teach her how to be both inside herself and outside and then to create a safe space in which to grow.

I will help my child discover who she is.

We are not trying to educate children and send them into the world as finished products — we send them forward as a person well begun.

Sr. Angela Boyo

Today I look at my children with wonder and gratitude. I know that you are not mine, that someday you will grow up and go, that even if you stayed, you would belong to yourselves and not to me. But you have awakened a corner of my slumbering soul that will never fall asleep again. You have opened a door in my heart and taught me how to see. I have love inside of me for you that I never knew was there. So no matter what might happen between us — no matter where your life might take you — you will live within me as a hidden treasure. Nothing can ever take it away.

A part of my heart will always be dedicated to you.

"The men where you live," said the little prince, "raise five thousand roses in the same garden — and they do not find in it what they are looking for. And yet what they are looking for could be found in one single rose or in a little water. But the eyes are blind. One must look with the heart . . ."

Antoine de St.-Exupery